CINDY LASS

CINDY LASS

A Colourful Pawtrait

BIOGRAPHY BY GINA CLARKE

Matador
Unit E2 Airfield Business Park,
Harrison Road, Market Harborough,
Leicestershire. LE16 7UL
Tel: 0116 2792299
Email: books@troubador.co.uk
Web: www.troubador.co.uk/matador
Twitter: @matadorbooks

ISBN 978 1800465 664

British Library Cataloguing in Publication Data.
A catalogue record for this book is available from the British Library.

Printed and bound in Great Britain by 4edge Limited
Typeset in 11pt Minion Pro by Troubador Publishing Ltd, Leicester, UK

Matador is an imprint of Troubador Publishing Ltd

DEDICATIONS

Gina Clarke

A huge thank you to my family and friends who have helped bring my work and home life into balance. I love you all.

Cindy Lass
I would like to dedicate this book to my darling mummy Jilly, whose love and determination got me to here. My father Jack who taught me self-respect and kept me safe. My supportive and wonderful husband Roger, our sons Ollie and Jack and my beloved but dearly departed doggie, Flash x

All Our Hearts Beat As One.

Colour is the appetite of life – it never changes.

By Cindy Lass, 2020.

AUTHOR'S NOTE

By Gina Clarke

When I first met Cindy in the basement bar of a hotel in London, I was almost a year into launching my career as a freelance journalist. As a busy mum of two, a forced redundancy had left an urgent need to get my career back on track, and so I embarked on a quest to work for myself and say 'yes' to everything for twelve months.

And so that night, I found a babysitter and hopped on the train. A collaboration between journalists, PRs and some celebs, I wasn't sure what I would find. And never in a million years did I expect to come across someone like Cindy. Not only did she know everyone (and always have a story or two to tell), things just seemed to happen to her. She would walk down the street and an opportunity or a chance meeting with a celebrity would simply arise. Immediately, I knew that if I was going to write a book about anyone, it would be about her.

Over the years we've become friends and having had her welcome me to her home as we worked on this book together, it has only cemented the feeling I had on that first night in a hot, stuffy bar in London that Cindy's story needed to be told.

And while this book has been years in the making, my only regret is that we would have had longer. With Cindy, there is always something happening, and I'm sure that this will not be the last we will hear from her, yet I hope this book might lead to a greater understanding of what she stands for and why art is so important to her.

From artist to entrepreneur with a charity-first attitude, Cindy has certainly been the colour in my life for the past few years while writing this book. I hope you enjoy reading it as much as I have enjoyed putting it together.

INTRODUCTION

By Cindy Lass

My name is Cindy Lass and I'm so glad you've decided to pick up and read this book. I'm not a writer, but I want to take a moment to put some energy down on this page so you can get to know the real me.

Everyone is vulnerable. Imagine you've just walked into a room of people, and you don't know who anyone is. Well, don't worry because I'm here and I'm striding across the floor ready to welcome you. You're going to really hear the warm 'hello' in my voice; I'm going to look you in the eye with a big smile and – if permitted – give you a quick hug because what I'm trying to say is that I want you here. I want you to read my story and I want you to bring every drop of your amazing consciousness and focus; because, quite frankly, we all need some positivity in our lives.

When I met Gina, we got together over drinks at a lovely little party opposite St Martin's Hotel in Soho. It was that instant connection that I described above. We were both drawn to each other, and she seemed to genuinely be interested in my stories. As my husband says, I can walk down the same road and nothing will ever happen to him and yet things just seem to happen to me.

I know that from Gina's point of view, my painting of the Queen's corgis plus my work with A-list celebs was a great starting point for a book. But actually, as we've spent time writing this together, I've realised that I want to use this opportunity not just to tell you about me – the little girl from Hampstead who became a famous artist by accident – but to start a conversation with you.

I've been a ballet dancer, actress, model and finally, a mother. That's where I thought I would stay – the pinnacle of my achievement. But we as people all have something else inside of us. Something more to give. It was like having a captured butterfly in my handbag; I could feel the essence of its ongoing vibration through its wings, the rhythm inside never seemed to dampen. And finally, I learned through my art to let it out to fly.

I really hope that this book will inspire you to find your creative side, whatever it might be or just give you the push to believe in your dreams. From dancing to painting, my life is not so much about finding success but finding my outlet. Sometimes I marvel that I actually make a living through doing something that gives me the greatest joy on earth. Other times, through deadlines or just the people I've met along the way, there's been a sense of urgency created that gives me a feeling of dread in the pit of my stomach.

But throughout my career, despite the financial or social repercussions, I've learned to follow my gut and appreciate who has my best interests at heart. Definitely my recently departed stunning mummy whose sayings were everything happens for a reason and when one door closes another one opens. Keep going. I believe we are all a part of Mother Earth's necklace, linked together but given the same space and raw ingredients, all of us belong here. I have a huge belief in the power of connection, after all, the Universe waters all the trees in the forest, it doesn't necessarily choose one or the other. To me, we are all the same. What I hope you'll take from this book is inspiration to find that bit of creativity inside of you, either deep down or bubbling away at the surface. But know that you must stay true to yourself, let go and believe in your passions.

After all, our lives are defined by our passion and self-belief. I've always had the ability to laugh at myself whatever the circumstance I've been through. So, think positive; enjoy this book; and get to know the real Cindy Lass – whoever she may be.

CONTENTS

CONTENTS

CONTENTS

CHAPTER 1

CHILDHOOD DREAMS: CINDY'S EARLY LIFE

Life in London

Cindy Lass was born in London, on the 14th of June 1964. The youngest child of Jack and Jill Grant, Cindy was thrust into the limelight at a young age – although curiously, her talent for art only became apparent later in life. She lived with her two older siblings, Tracy and Craig, in a house Jack had designed and built on The Bishops Avenue in Hampstead. A leafy part of London, Cindy's early days were spent in a lovely little cul-de-sac called White Lodge Close. Modern before its time, Cindy's home was open plan with a huge garden – perfect for her socialite parents to entertain, as they often did. While her surroundings may have been the envy of most, Cindy later realised that behind closed doors were some very dysfunctional families – her own included.

Her father, Jack Grant, was originally born Lionel Goorwich but before marrying her mother changed it to Grant on the insistence of his new bride. Jill had tried out the name by ringing the butcher's shop one day to place an order and found that no-one could spell it over the phone. Only the name change wasn't just for Jack, as Jill also required it to include all seven of his siblings. Knowing how much he loved her, they agreed.

As well as coming from a large family, Cindy confirms that her father was the most handsome. A boxer in his youth, it earned him the nickname 'Jack the Horse'. But his time in the ring wouldn't last long as by the age of fourteen he had started a successful menswear wholesale business in London's East End, famous for its clothing markets. Thanks to his success, Jack was able to look after much of his extended family – one of the reasons why he remained the favourite of his mother Millie, who also ran her own business.

Jill was an elegant but formidable woman who truly shaped the course of the family, and who was one of Cindy's biggest supporters. What's more, her influence can be found throughout Cindy's career. From the first blue vase painting that accidentally led to gallery owner Barbara Grundy discovering her talents, to the famous Grant name change.

Cindy describes her early childhood as 'happy-go-lucky', where a sensitive young girl grew up to love dancing, needlepoint and even maths. Still, as she got older, Cindy remembers that the atmosphere was often tense between her parents, and from the age of nine she experienced regular arguments as the couple almost separated on a number of occasions. As a distraction, the Grant children turned to creative outlets to see them through the drama, and both

2

ballet and bike rides with her brother were a welcome relief to Cindy. These memories are interspersed by fond moments with her parents. Gardening with Jack while shopping with Jill, who received her good sense from her own mother (who only died at 102 after health complications). Jill was also behind a lot of Cindy's creative endeavours, taking her modelling at three years old where Cindy remembers being called a 'stunning doll' – although this reference was something she hated. Overall, she admits to being spoiled by both parents, being the youngest and the apple of their eye. As a youngster no expense would be spared including large, amazing birthday parties of up to forty children in the garden with a top-class entertainer, where her mum would cheer her on.

It's therefore unsurprising that Cindy has never been one to prefer a slower pace of life, but in order to sustain such energy and enthusiasm, Cindy has always craved a firm grounding. First with family, and then good friends before she eventually settled down. Surrounding herself with good people allows Cindy the freedom to think differently, and in turn, become more receptive to opportunities when they present themselves. But it could have been so very different.

Finding Her Feet at Annemount

One of Cindy's earliest memories is of her first day in school, joining the nursery at Annemount Pre-preparatory School in Hampstead, watching everyone rush by and thinking, *what's the hurry?* She remembers other children struggling to learn the alphabet while she was already ahead and onto the next thing. Still, she soon settled down into a routine and young Cindy would go from playing nicely in the little school garden, to getting home just in time for her glamorous mum to sweep in from a luncheon or charity event. It was Jill's preference to indulge in such pastimes, and while never a typical mother, her dedication to charity was something that was instilled in Cindy at a young age.

Still, aged just five, she was deemed too intelligent for Annemount and moved early (most children stayed until the age of seven) to the larger Henrietta Barnett School in Hampstead Garden Suburbs. This was incredibly scary for young Cindy and something she wasn't happy about. She remembers that the big halls and classrooms were all very different to her cosy life at Annemount, and her report that year admitted that *Cindy is a very clever little girl however, she gets upset very quickly at the slightest mishap*.

Mishaps aside, it was here that Cindy formed a relationship with art and physical education. The PE teacher there was called Mrs Jarvis, who was simply an angel to Cindy – and perhaps the first in a long line of people who have spent time developing and nurturing Cindy's unique skill sets, although this wasn't something she fully comprehended at this age. One fond memory Cindy has is of earning house merit points for her dancing interpretations in PE lessons. Such an achievement was cause for celebration as she would never receive merit points in her traditional classes. On Mrs Jarvis' recommendation, Cindy joined the Russian ballet school aged nine years old, which Jill hoped would strengthen her small-framed daughter's back and legs.

A Love for Ballet

It was here she met ballerina Natasha Lisakova, an Australian daughter of a war veteran, who ran the London Classical Ballet School at an old church hall in Golders Green. Cindy found Natasha delightful and was keen to learn – not just about the ballet, but in her home life too, especially since Natasha had two daughters herself. Jill wasn't the best at timekeeping – forever late, sometimes even up to two hours – so Cindy, Natasha and her daughters spent a lot of time together.

Perhaps unsurprisingly, Natasha was quick to spot Cindy's talent and introduced the young student to Bloch shoes. Six months later, she received honours in her ballet exam due to the 'great elevation' in her jumps. Cindy admits:

> "I credit Natasha with my love of ballet – despite the three stern-looking examiners, when the music started, I just went into another zone – I loved it."

Suddenly, with the news that her parents had a ballerina on their hands, lessons went from just one afternoon after school in a dusty hall, to five or more a week. At the age of eleven years old, Cindy auditioned for, and won, a place at the famous Bolshoi Ballet in Russia. For her father Jack, the prospect of his little girl training each day on her own in a country far away simply was not going to happen, despite his pride in her ability. Cindy's view was that he thought *no way is this 4ft 9in skinny daughter of mine going to Russia by herself.* With days full of training non-stop each day, Jack was of the opinion that it would have been a hard life for Cindy,

5

so she didn't go. Still, lessons with Natasha were incredibly valuable as she made Cindy believe in herself, beginning a love for music – enjoying moving her body to the rhythm and the release that can still make her feel alive today, although in truth, the constant lessons meant her feet suffered from an early age; she developed two hook toes that have never been the same since.

Des O'Connor

In one respect, the ballet gave Cindy her first taste of life as a celebrity through both putting on performances and dressing up for the occasion. True to life, Cindy always has a story to tell, and one performance was quick to cause a stir. A very good-looking, well-turned-out man appeared one night to watch an end-of-term performance. Despite the hot weather outside he arrived wearing oversized sunglasses and a huge scarf – Mr. Inconspicuous! She had heard other students asking school friends Samantha and Tracy O'Connor if their dad would be in attendance but didn't realise that he was actually the well-known TV star Des O'Connor who had his own talk-show.

It wouldn't be until years later that she spotted this huge star of the screen and realised she had performed in front of him without even realising! Typical Cindy, later in her career she would constantly be around celebrities but was never phased by their glamour – she would simply think:

"Well we all have to go to the toilet".

The Challenges of Secondary School

With the ballet out of the picture, Jill had another problem on her hands – where would Cindy go to secondary school? Despite having a natural intelligence and creative talent, Cindy had a secret – she was no good with reading. Today, she would have been diagnosed with dyslexia, but at the time she was simply made to practice more often.

She remembers a truly embarrassing moment while at Henrietta Barnett aged nine years old and studying English. Chosen by the teacher to read aloud from her own work, an essay that she was mightily proud of, Cindy's brain raced ahead and she skipped a whole paragraph, rendering the rest of the episode slightly nonsensical. Cindy's embarassment grew as she couldn't find her way back. All the while her classmates clapped their hands over their faces, trying to stifle their laughter. Even now when Cindy struggles to find the right word, she can hear the peals of laughter, and the tips of her ears still turn bright red at the memory. She desperately wanted the ground to swallow her up as no matter how hard she looked, the paragraph she needed had disappeared. Such is the pain of Cindy's dyslexia, the words simply fade away.

The laughter of the other students and anger of the teacher resonated deeply throughout the rest of her time at the school – she felt embarrassed and belittled, which only made her steer away from academic interests. It is something she still struggles with today, misreading or writing things down backwards – as her eyes and brain, when tired or stressed, simply do not work in sync. Words and symbols (especially the @ sign in today's technology-driven world) can easily get missed out.

These days, Cindy has accepted her dyslexia and, if once she was frustrated at herself, now she wears her badge of acceptance proudly and is happy to speak up and let people know that she is different. Although, she does tend to get mixed reactions – some say, 'oh, that's a good excuse' when she asks for help to fill out a form, or others just think she is lazy. Cindy worries sometimes,

"It's amazing how horrible we human beings can be to each other."

After her embarrassing episode in class, Jack's decision to refuse the Russian Ballet's offer meant that the young girl who was scared of academia now faced the entrance exam for the Henrietta Barnett Upper School. While her acceptance would have made Jill's morning commute much easier (Cindy's older sister already had a place there) Cindy found to her horror that whether it was her dyslexia or she had perhaps misunderstood the assignment, the English Comprehension entrance paper wasn't something she understood at all. It was no surprise that she failed the exam and lost her place at the school.

She remembers not engaging with the text in the examination hall, looking around as others studiously worked while barely writing a word herself. While not planned, it seemed to be a glimpse of Cindy's future attitude to studies, as though she knew the school system in its current form wasn't for her. She says:

"The whole experience was so intense. I remember a wooden floor in the classroom with the smell of polish – there was a scary lady sitting behind her desk in a skirt suit looking incredibly serious, as if my life depended on this one exam. To me, at that age, it was ridiculous."

Luckily, an eccentric friend of Jill's called Liz who lived nearby to them in Hampstead village with two sweet Yorkshire terriers, suggested that Cindy should go to acting school. It would come with the possibility of gaining an Equity card, something which would later become important. To Cindy, Liz was one of her angels as from this one conversation she was able to set off on the right path. And so, a hurried audition for The Italia Conti Academy of Theatre Arts was organised. While her father was horrified – he didn't believe that acting, or any career in the arts, was a valid option and would lead Cindy to a miserable life – it didn't stop the audition from taking place. Unsurprisingly, Cindy passed with flying colours and should have gone on to join a year group that included Bonnie Langford and Lena Zavaroni, but with the turbulence at home, eleven-year-old Cindy didn't feel comfortable with a sharp turn into acting so soon after her career in ballet had been dashed. Both parents also knew that the academic demands of the school would be hard on Cindy. There were some very high standards of education to adhere to that just wouldn't fit in with the type of child that Cindy was becoming. It was time to look elsewhere.

Finding Herself at Corona Academy

Luckily Liz once again came to the rescue, suggesting the Corona Academy in West London.

The school already had a prestigious history of producing young talent for both stage and screen, indeed, providing most of the cast of Lionel Bart's *Oliver*. Cindy remembers walking into her audition and feeling like the place was home; children from all walks of life just appeared to have landed there, and for Cindy this eclectic blend would lead to life-long friendships and many opportunities along the way. While waiting to hear if there was a space for young Cindy, Jill was worried – what would they do if the answer was 'no'? She had already told Cindy that mothers could go to prison if their child didn't go to school, something which played heavily on the eleven-year old's mind. Knowing that Jill was running out of options made Cindy nervous, especially ahead of her admissions interview but Joan Tandy from Corona understood the situation, allaying her nerves somewhat. Thankfully it was a resounding yes, as the last time Cindy had seen Jill look this scared was when she took her to have a brace fitted in Finchley Road, North London. The dentist had said that Cindy had no lower back teeth in the left corner of her jaw. It led to an operation at Middlesex hospital aged eleven, where Jill had to sign a consent form to allow the team to work deep into the jawbone, with a chance that Cindy could be permanently disfigured. She will never forget seeing the look of pain on her mother's face after the operation, not realising it was a way for Jill to keep in check her horror of the surgery. Luckily, all went well, and Cindy has normal function in her mouth today.

Cindy was accepted to start in September and is still thankful to Joan for her calming influence to this day. She cannot remember one academic day in all the years she spent there, only that it was fantastic for a child like her – full of energy but with no knowledge of how to channel it in a conventional way. Corona was not there to repress Cindy's spirit for life, it was there to enhance it.

The first week that Cindy attended, she found herself filming with actor Gregory Peck and actress Lee Remick. Her dad Jack later went to the premiere but he came back green and, once recovered, said, *"Promise me you'll never watch it!"* The film was the notorious horror flick, *The Omen*, with Harvey Stephens playing demon child Damien. Cindy has stayed true to her word, and to this day has never seen the cult movie.

With other notable actors from school, albeit differing year groups, including Nicholas Lyndhurst of *Only Fools and Horses* and Lisa Vanderpump from *The Real Housewives of Beverly Hills*, Corona should have been a success for Cindy from day one. But with two hundred kids thrown in together from all walks of life, those early months weren't exactly a bed of roses for a child like her.

That first journey on the London tube by herself seemed exotic for pre-teen Cindy, only 4ft 9in, and dressed in the school uniform of yellow socks and a green tunic. The only complication was her hat; she had to wear a rather large and unflattering green felt hat with a yellow band on the train to and from the school each day. The students were told that people would be watching on the journey to make sure that children wore it correctly (which led to Cindy being constantly on the lookout for these so-called uniform police). In the summer the unattractive green felt was replaced by an equally large and unattractive summer boater.

Each morning Cindy caught the tube from East Finchley, a 30-minute walk from Cindy's house in White Lodge Close.

She would then have to spend an hour underground at each end to navigate her way to and from the academy. A route that many would consider unthinkable now for such a young girl. Yet from eleven this was to be her new journey each day. But it became something she both loved – getting to experience the sights and sounds of London – and loathed, as it was a journey she had to take by herself. Cindy had to grow up quickly as it wasn't always kind people who shared her space; although she is quick to brush off some of the more difficult experiences, Cindy had her fair share of dealing with men who exposed themselves to the schoolgirl or made her feel awkward – an early lesson in staying wary of others and always following your intuition.

For the first six weeks of term, Cindy had yet to find her voice and was picked on and bullied by some of the students. To everyone else, she was a middle-class Jew living in Millionaire's Row, only she didn't follow the stereotype. Indeed, she didn't actually realise her prosperity until friends from Corona would come over. While she had previously heard the area referred to as Millionaire's Row, it wasn't something she dwelled on. But when Jill served salmon and cucumber finger sandwiches to her council estate friends, comments such as *"Ooh very la-di-dah"* and *"Your Wendy house is bigger than my flat!"* began to make their way into Cindy's subconscious. She soon realised that not everyone was as fortunate. What fascinated Cindy was that students at Corona came from all walks of life but still all got on like one happy family. Soon they all became friends and they would meet up locally on an evening or go to a greasy spoon called Nick's café twenty yards from the school. Cindy loved it there as it had a space invaders machine which in the

1980s would let you play for hours for the princely sum of ten pence.

Like most from Corona, Cindy practically lived at Nick's – it gave the students an opportunity to share their unique stories. If not in the café, you could find the gang playing together on the tree outside the Academy. Spending every day together soon became the norm, despite a lot of students finding success while still at school or having famous parents. Getting to know the children of the teachers was also not unexpected. Cindy remembers Anne Kettle, who as well as teaching Cindy to sing was also the lady who made sure that everyone was in the appropriate attire, whether fitting a new leotard or a lost straw boater, her commitment to the school meant that her son often had to accompany her most afternoons while she worked. That little boy was Paul Bettany, who is now renowned for playing Vision in the Marvel Cinematic Universe, involved in films such as *Iron Man*, *The Avengers* and *Captain America*. But Cindy's memories are a little different. She laughs:

> "I remember Paul as a skinny boy of eight who would just be hanging with us, running around the playground waiting for his mum to take him home and make the tea. His dad, Thane Bettany – also an actor – used to teach us Shakespeare and I absolutely loved his class."

Yet the responsibility of acting and touring was constantly felt on such young shoulders, Cindy's included. Putting on a play for the younger members of a school on one such tour, the very serious third scene went awry as a stray ashtray clonked one of the actors on the nose, who somehow managed to finish his lines despite a steady stream of blood continuing to dribble out.

The owner of the school, Miss Rona Knight, would say that laughing on stage during a serious performance, or corpsing, was equal to sinning on stage, but during this episode Cindy couldn't help it. She and other members of the crew found themselves attacked by a fit of the giggles thanks to the unexpected interruption. Yet when the cast traipsed backstage after the show, it was Cindy that Miss Knight singled out. While she had tried so much to keep it in, Cindy had laughed with the rest of them and now Miss Knight looked her straight in the eye and said, *"Out of everyone I thought I could rely on you Cindy not to corpse"* Still a teenager at the time, it was the worst Cindy had ever felt in her life, and is something she will never forget – or repeat, even to this day.

Through shared experiences such as this, no matter the past or where they are now, the students of Corona became her 'soulmates' and many are still in touch today. Not only do they talk daily through social media such as Facebook, but the gang regularly meet up when times allow.

After she turned fifteen, Jack and Jill made the decision to move into a prestigious apartment block, Bryanston Court in Marble Arch. This dramatically cut down Cindy's commuting time, although it was a little strange leaving one house in the morning and finding her way to a completely different address in the afternoon.

Learning Her Way Around the Film Set

Corona also played a big part in Cindy's career, as through the school, she gained the occasional acting assignment, commercials and radio voice-overs. After her first taste of acting, Cindy was encouraged by the stage school to help out with other movies that were being filmed. Glenda Jackson was another star that she spent time with on the set of *The Incredible Sarah*, a British dramatisation of the acting career of Sarah Bernhardt – although the actress wasn't keen on having too much to do with the schoolchildren on set.

Cindy learned very quickly to keep her head down around A-list celebrities, alongside her chaperone. It was very apparent to her how strange these people were, changing their personas so quickly depending on the person they were talking to.

When she was twelve, Cindy was one of the extras filming *Jesus of Nazareth* for the BBC. While actor Robert Powell played Jesus, Cindy's role was less in the spotlight. Alongside other children dressed as angels with wings on, she had to stand on a raised block for a long time. Despite having strict rules around filming with young people, the scenes regularly went on past 5pm and Cindy remembers sitting around all day, which was exhausting for an exuberant child. Still, when it came on TV her mum Jill rushed out to buy the *Radio Times*. She was very proud of her youngest daughter, but while Cindy appreciated the recognition, she also knew how difficult it had been with the long hours, make-up and wardrobe. It was then that Cindy realised she didn't want a career where she would be sat around all day, waiting to be part of something. Acting was a double-edged sword; while she loved the people she met and the parts she got to play, the actual process was a nightmare for the energetic young girl.

What Cindy started to crave was a role with stability. Not just turning up for a day or two at a time, but something she could sink her teeth into, even star in. Her first attempt for a TV series came with a casting call for Enid Blyton's intrepid adventurers, *The Famous Five*. One of her favourite books, this was a challenge Cindy relished. But it wasn't to be. Instead of feeling dejected, she poured all her energy into the next key role that came along – this time for the made-for-television film biopic of Israeli Prime Minister, Golda Meir. The film was called *A Woman Called Golda*, released in 1982 and starring Ingrid Bergman, who Cindy met at her audition. She made it down to the final two for the role, and spent a lot of time with the director and producer as they whittled down their casting process. Ultimately, Cindy lost out. When she heard the news, Cindy felt like her world had ended. To be so close to something but not to play a part – it's a feeling Cindy thinks many children these days experience when looking at social media. A heart-wrenching feeling from the realisation that they have been deliberately excluded from an event, but then go on to scrutinise each picture of their friends having fun.

Short-term, adverts became a focus for the young Cindy. The filming wrapped much more quickly and the instant appeal of seeing herself on TV or in a magazine was gratifying. Still, she was learning about how the industry works along the way. The same year after her *Famous Five* disappointment, she played a main role in a Dulux paint commercial. It was here she realised how much advertising was all a trick of the eye. Together, the students from Corona would run into a room with their hands full of mud, which they took great pleasure in smearing over a wall. The advert was meant to showcase how easy it was to wipe clean new paint, only the final version was shot with soot on the walls, which was much easier to wipe off. Understanding the smoke and mirrors that went into such effects, Cindy learned to trust her gut and know when something, or someone, felt off.

Still, there was an upside to shooting such commercials. One for car company Austin, as it launched its Mini Metro, saw Cindy flying to Brussels and Dusseldorf, where she was put in a literal robotic suit which was then screwed shut. This claustrophobic chamber was a nightmare to get in and out of, even for a slip of a girl like Cindy. With electrics on the front she could barely see what she was doing, anxiously listening for "Action" and "Cut". An experience that still terrifies her, and something she would in no way repeat now, yet there was a small compensation of travelling with a chaperone to five-star hotels that helped to make up for the role. As did the great people she met, plus the money was very good.

At this point in life, Cindy's relationship with her mother was becoming more highly-strung as the youngster became a teenager. Still, the power of parenthood should never be underestimated and Cindy remembers storming on to the plane getting ready to fly to Belgium after an argument with Jill. Settled in her economy seat, the captain came over the tannoy, *"Can a Cindy Grant please come forward, we can't take off until we speak to you"*. Absolutely mortified she remembers walking to the cockpit at the front of the plane, past all the watching eyes in Business Class, where the captain added, *"We've just had a call from your mother to say she's sorry, and she wishes you a great flight."* Heartened, but still incredibly embarrassed, Cindy returned to her seat to ponder how Jill had even managed to get through to the pilot of the plane?

Still, life lessons were never far away and as children from the stage school were regulars in BBC plays, one such appearance stands out. It was 1980 and Cindy was taking part in the BBC production of the 19th century melodrama, *Maria Marten* – otherwise known as *Murder in the Red Barn*. She was in a rehearsal room on location the size of a football pitch, much too big to feel very involved in the actual filming, and instead was reading a book when the director came across, snatched the book away and shouted, *"In my day, we watched everything that goes on when on the rehearsal stage!"* Cindy was shocked into silence, as was her chaperone and everyone around her. It was a horrible experience for the young teenager but one which she continues to reflect on. To this day, unless she is in a green room, Cindy sits and watches everything that happens – and to the angry director's credit, she believes she has learned a lot.

There was also a short foray into singing; Cindy was asked to audition for a new musical – *Annie* – and while she gamely sang *Happy Birthday* ten times for her audition, the verdict was that her voice just wasn't strong enough.

Another failed singing attempt was an audition through the Pineapple agency, aged 17. Cindy had to attend the Queen's Theatre in Covent Garden and sing *Don't Rain on my Parade* from *Funny Girl*. While Cindy classes herself as, *"not a great singer, I'm a bit tone deaf but a great dancer"*, she still values feedback. Especially after going to the effort of turning up for an audition, even borrowing someone else's Bloch shoes to hit the right movements, a big no-no in dancing as it was like wearing someone else's feet. When finished, a voice in the dark theatre shouted *"Next!"* But Cindy remained on the stage – *"No, no, no"* she said as she stood her ground. *"I would like some criticism"*. After a moment's pause the voice came back, sounding surprised to be asked. *"Your actions are good, your dancing is good but your voice just isn't strong enough. But it was a good audition."*

For Cindy, relieved that she now wouldn't need the Bloch shoes any more, this was worth the effort of learning a new song and dance, and she left the stage singing with a smile on her face. As she passed other performers warming up at the side of the stage they thought she had got through to the next round, but Cindy just smiled, *"No, I'm going home"*. They all looked at her like she had gone slightly mad – but professional feedback at this stage in her career was just as good as any new role.

While she clearly looked the part and could dance and act, Cindy accepted that singing just wasn't to be. But there was still no thought on the horizon of a definitive plan. Her timetable still revolved around ballet dancing and other creative pursuits – essentially, she was waiting for a big starry role to come along and decide her future. Only it never did. Still relatively untrained in art and doubting her own abilities, Cindy decided to take the easy way out when it came to art class. A decision she has never told anyone and still regrets to this day. Cindy explains what happened at the time:

"I finished school with an A in spoken English and went on to gain three O-levels, alongside a painful U in French. While today I might be a well-known artist, back then I didn't have a clue who I was or what I might be good at. When it came to my art exam, I'm ashamed to say (and have never previously admitted) that the work wasn't my own.

"A friend of my dad's, who used to work in one of his shops, offered me his sketch one day. It was beautiful and showed a man lying peacefully under a tree. Although clearly not my style right now, at the time I would have loved to have said it was mine, and to my shame, that's exactly what I did. During the rest of the course, I felt unhappy and uninspired, leading to my overall art grade falling to a D. It is something I am ashamed of to this day. Still, it taught me humility. And that is a trait I am proud to carry with me. I believe that in some way, it was all meant to happen, and these were simply lessons I had to learn at the time."

The London Scene and Meeting David Bowie

In her final years at Corona, Cindy's acting and dancing abilities were in high demand as blockbuster hits continued to be filmed locally in London. Cindy was a regular at both Shepperton and Elstree Studios and even filmed on location in central London when required.

Cindy also featured in the film *Return to Oz*, which was released in 1985 by Disney as a sequel to the incredibly successful 1939 movie starring Judy Garland, *The Wizard of Oz*. Cindy was a dancer on the set and in early spring 1984, would drive her car to Elstree studios in the dark each morning to be on set for 3am. A typical Gemini, she would come home exhausted but get up bright and early to do it all again the next day. But while quickly making friends with the make-up artists, eating delicious sausage rolls and having a ball with the rest of the cast, the director Walter Murch and producer Gary Kurtz, faced a much more difficult time.

While Disney owned the rights to nearly all the books in the *Oz* series, the first book, *The Wonderful Wizard of Oz*, was still with the original studios, MGM. Which meant that *Return to Oz* was actually an amalgamation of two subsequent books in the series and was imagined as a much darker production in tone than before. This wasn't always easy to translate on camera and made for a stressful set. Cindy remembers on one occasion with a variety of mirrors used in shot, it became hard to film without seeing the reflection of a camera. The air turned blue with swear words – and even to a tried and tested crew, the atmosphere was unbearable. It meant that the extras were cut by two-thirds, and Cindy was one of the few that came back to re-shoot the scene once a solution had been identified.

When Disney eventually arrived on set to take stock, Kurtz was moved to another role with new producer Paul Maslansky hired to work with Murch, who himself was fired as the director when filming ran a week behind schedule, just four weeks into production. He was subsequently re-hired on the personal request of George Lucas.

During her time at Corona, Cindy remembers filming with a famous American actor who had played Atticus Finch in the 1962 drama film *To Kill a Mockingbird*. The next week, during a large wedding she attended with family, she was asked who was starring in the film. Remembering *"an old man called Gregory Peck"*, Jill was horrified when Cindy unknowingly described her screen idol as old – after all, he was still good-looking to her. But the glamour of the showbiz industry soon lost its lustre for Cindy, as there was a lot of waiting around for a teenage star-struck girl – although students from the school were told to be polite and not stare and that any celebrities were to be treated the same as other people. Due in part to all those hours spent on set, to this day, Cindy still doesn't see anyone from an A-list star to a waitress any differently.

Yet there was one occasion that Cindy will always remember: her introduction to David Bowie in 1985, who she says was *"one of the coolest and most handsome stars I have ever met"*. She was cast as a dancer with three other girls in the film *Absolute Beginners*, released in 1986, where Bowie's character, Vendice Partners sings *That's Motivation*. The sequence was a complicated one which featured dancing on a revolving record player while Colin, played by Eddie O'Connell, is lowered down on a motorbike. The stunt mesmerised Cindy every time the camera started rolling and made her forget the lyrics three times – leading to the cut of her closeup. Still, Cindy didn't mind; she can still be seen clearly dancing to the left of Bowie during the wide shots of the scene and will always have the memories of those two special weeks at Elstree studios.

While typically cast as an dancer, Cindy was used to being seen but not heard by the talent. But straight away Bowie made it clear that things would be very different where he was concerned. He made a beeline for the gang of dancers during a break in filming, sitting on the large typewriter used in another sequence while his fellow actors headed back to the green room. Although co-star Patsy Kensit did comment on Cindy's long legs. She was very sweet, the pair had a chat about her life and she left complimenting Cindy's nails saying she wished hers were as nice. But with Bowie, Cindy was struck by David's charisma and energy – a first impression like no other. Despite being dressed in nothing but a skimpy bikini with records glued on and a pink wig, Bowie made her feel incredibly comfortable. Yet also for the first time in her life, speechless. She remembers,

"He had two different coloured eyes that felt like they could see into my soul. I was aware of how his kindness and angelic soul came through. Being so close to him with the four of us on this huge typewriter, we looked like idiots really but he made it clear he would rather be with us than the other VIPs. He always had time to chat; I've since met many stars but none had such a quality as him. That experience with him was really a turning point when I look back.

"I then bumped into him again at an airport a few years later. He was sitting in the lounge and smiled. He just had this amazing presence and aura. When I heard he had died I felt very shocked and sad, like so many others whose lives he touched."

Although the film was not a commercial success, Bowie's song *Absolute Beginners* became one of the most successful singles of the 1980s in the UK, reaching No. 2 in the charts.

Jack and Jill Decide to Divorce

Life on stage and screen wasn't always as glamorous as it might be portrayed. Towards the end of her time at Corona, Cindy

was performing in the play *Equus*, a school production –
playing the stable girl Jill Mason, a role which meant she had
to simulate having sex on stage. This was quite embarrassing
because back then, everyone on set had experienced sex but
Cindy and what's more, they all knew it. It was made worse
by looking out in the auditorium and seeing the faces of her
parents, albeit at individual times. By this point, the pair
were going through a bad patch.

Friends were her lifeline when tensions between her
parents began to spill over and divorce became imminent.
While the decision was unbearable for Jack, he knew it was
the right thing to do for Jill. Despite the difficulties between
the couple, Cindy remembers spending more time with her
dad as he began semi-retirement. She says:

> "Like all families, we had our ups and downs, and it
> was difficult on one hand as it wasn't easy for either
> of them."

When the separation and divorce proceedings eventually
began, Cindy felt as though the rug had been pulled out
from under her feet. Jack moved out with Cindy's brother
to a new place in Regent's Park while Cindy and Jill moved
to a new apartment in Holland Park after the sale of
Bryanston Court; there was a very chilly six months where
the father and daughter struggled to talk. Jack was of the
opinion that Cindy was taking Jill's side, especially as the
family resemblance between Jill and Cindy was becoming
more apparent.

This was a horrible time for Cindy, who was already
struggling with her sister at university – happy in her own

relationship – and her brother now both in business with Jack and living with him, which meant she hardly got to see him. Despite initially not wanting to divorce, once he realised there was no other option that could change Jill's mind Jack represented himself in court during the actual divorce proceedings and told the female judge that, actually, he wasn't interested in giving Jill's lawyer any more money because he still loved her very much and was going to make sure she was well looked after.

While Jill settled down with another partner later in life, Harold, Cindy believes that Jack loved her mum until his death almost twenty years later.

Another key realisation for Cindy was when she ventured over to Washington D.C. aged around eighteen years old on a trip with friends. While attending a sit-down dinner during an outing at a country club, her first time at such an event, the young man she had been seated next to was very keen to chat about how individuals needed a certain amount of money in the bank before they became members. Cindy hates this sort of talk, and would rather the subject of money wasn't mentioned.

Watching the club's female members float around in their diamonds and pearls, Cindy looked down at her own outfit, a little black dress with the small pieces of gold jewellery she had acquired over the years. She was quick to notice that the young buck wasn't quite looking in her eyes, more at the bangles and rings she had on. He asked, *"So, what does your father do?"* To Cindy that was a red flag, she immediately put together that it meant – "So, what are you worth?" Keeping it light and managing still to speak with a straight face she said, *"Well at the moment he's working out how to put two farts in a jar and he wants me to design the labels on it."* Shocked, the man turned away and didn't speak to Cindy for the rest of the night – and for that Cindy was relieved.

Happy Memories in the Flower Shop

Cindy stayed on at Corona until she was eighteen years old, but after her final school production of *Guys and Dolls*, it led to a fairly frank conversation between father and daughter. Jack, although proud and keen to support Cindy, made it clear he would only continue to help Cindy further her career in the arts and continue to live rent-free if she got a part-time job to help herself along the way. Being respectful, knowing the value of money and earning your way was important to the man who made his way from wholesaler to businessman.

Cindy had grown up working Saturdays in a busy shop with her father, as the boss's daughter there were no lunch breaks or other perks which meant that going back to this wasn't something she wanted to do. One day, on her way home she noticed a gorgeous pink shop that looked deliciously inviting. As she looked in the window she saw gorgeous flower arrangements and tempting chocolates – the smell was simply devine. Cindy knew that if she would have to work anywhere, then something like this would be top of her list. Within a few weeks, she had her first part-time job, working for Graham Swabe and his manageress Julie every Friday and Saturday at Georgies, the pink chocolate shop and florist in St John's Wood.

Her favourite task by far was dressing the windows with fabulous displays and making chocolate platters, but she would also serve the customers and make them tea. Her talents in the shop included chatting to the customers – which she loved – and taking up to three orders at once.

Her day would often consist of her tearing herself in two as she played the roles of both shop assistant and therapist. But Cindy loved listening to the customers; hearing about their problems grounded her. And she learned that everything could be made better with a cup of tea. Her natural love of Georgies meant that even though Cindy had no marketing experience, she was able to 'sell-in' opportunities for the company at top events. From up-market hotels to the car company Mercedes-Benz, she persuaded them that if they needed flowers and chocolates to offer with each sold car, Georgies was the place to come to. Gradually coming to understand her worth, Cindy asked for 10% of each 'deal', and found herself in a new, dazzling world of marketing. This part of Cindy's career, the knowledge that she felt she 'could' do something, even if she wasn't quite sure what 'it' was, has cemented the path Cindy took as an artist – where pure faith was often the only reason to continue on her path.

Still, it wasn't all rosy at the flower shop. Cindy remembers coming into work one Friday after a delivery the previous day. The flowers on show were stunning, so fresh and attractive. When an older gentleman came in with his wife later that day, Cindy took time to go through all the arrangements she could put together at short notice, as the pair were seeing their daughter the next day and wanted something beautiful to take with them. After speaking with Cindy the pair left an order worth £50–£75, worth twice as much today, ready to be sent the next day.

Little did Cindy know as she left for home later that day, that instead of using the fresh flowers out on the counter, Graham had used the older flowers which had been placed out of sight in the back. The next day, the gentleman came in again and as Cindy greeted him he told her truthfully how bitterly disappointed he was in the arrangement that had arrived. Not only were the flowers half dead, but he felt betrayed by Cindy's kindness and would never use the shop again despite Cindy offering him a full refund – which would have come out of her own money.

But fate has a strange way of bringing people back together. A year or so down the line, Jill surprised Cindy with the news that she was seeing someone. As they talked in the kitchen at Jill's new apartment in Holland Park, she had moved not long after Cindy finished school aged 18, Jill explained that the mystery man was waiting to meet Cindy in the lounge, and it sounded like he might know her already. Of course, the man was no other than Harold Laurier, the gentleman from the flower shop who received the old flowers. His wife had died not long after and by co-incidence, eventually he had bumped into Jill in Regent's Park and they had both hit it off.

The pair went over the flower shop episode with Harold revealing that as Cindy had spoken so passionately and eloquently about the arrangements, he believed that she must have been the owner. Had he realised otherwise he would never have been so harsh. Cindy also apologised for the shop's bad form, albeit without her knowledge, and the pair continued a friendship that lasted for another twenty-four years until Harold passed away.

Opportunity Knocks – Or Not

And while there was the odd headache at Georgies, truth be told, it suited Cindy to work part-time around her auditions and what's more, it was flower arranging that led Cindy to her first experience of being transported to another, simpler place – something she now uses her art for. At this point in her life, Cindy's family were happy to support her ventures, although they teasingly pointed out that she had *'more front than Brighton pier'* when putting herself forward for opportunities.

It was during this time that Cindy began to enjoy her own routines. Together with her girlfriends, one ritual was to go and browse Marylebone high street which she loved, before having their nails done at a boutique nail salon on Crawford Street. At the time there was a small gallery opposite and while waiting for appointments Cindy would go in and browse. Chatting to the gallerist, Cindy would put her new marketing skills to the test when it was clear the place struggled for an audience. From ringing up the local newspapers to drumming up friends, she was picking up tips and techniques that would stand her in good stead for her future career as an artist.

Still, like all young women desperate to make it on their own, Cindy took risks that, looking back now, had plenty of red flags. At one point, MTV were looking for a new presenter and confident that she could do the job, Cindy went along on a day off from Georgies, only to be turned away at the door – *"Sorry"* said the young chap manning the clipboard, *"The interview is only for blondes."* Cheekily adding with a wink, *"If you come back tomorrow as a blonde we might consider you.*" Naïve and keen for her big break, Cindy went over to buy a wig and set about trimming it to match her hairline. The next day, dressed in a matching woollen Joseph Tricot knitted jacket and skirt that Cindy described as 'chi-chi', complete with high heels, she got in her car and set off back to the interview.

But at this point in time, the late 1980s when Cindy was still living at Bryanston Court in Marble Arch, problems with IRA bombers were regular items on the news. It was only 9am, but on her route the police pulled Cindy's car over, and as she got out the policeman gave her such a look – he wasn't sure if she was a bomber or a prostitute! Despite having a rather embarrassing out of body experience, seeing herself dressed up in a blonde wig, miniskirt, and high heels by the side of the road, Cindy was able to carry on with her journey. But after another ninety-minute wait and a desperate attempt at styling the itchy blonde wig, the answer was still no. These sorts of instances hardened the young Cindy and now she embraces the passion and flow of painting, with a firm belief that you have to get through the bad stuff to understand what it means when things do go right.

An Early Career in Hand Modelling

While her career as a presenter was still to take off, at this point Cindy still only worked part-time, which allowed her to say yes to other exciting challenges, such as hand modelling and voice-overs. These proved to be lucrative and what's more, didn't take up too much time. This diversion in her career stemmed after a conversation with a friend who mentioned she had good hands and that it was a great way to make extra money. Her first job was a risqué scene shot at Pinewood Studios where she played the hands of Jamie Lee Curtis in *A Fish Called Wanda*.

Cindy's square nail bed luckily matched Jamie's, and the scene was reshot in post-production with Cindy stroking a photo and Jamie's voice imitating an orgasm in the background! Cindy, who is very hard to embarrass, laughs when recalling this memory.

> "I must say, life was never dull. At Henrietta Barnett, we were told that the word boredom does not belong in the English language, and I can honestly say I never use it. Sometimes I say, *'I'm tired'* or *'this is dull'*, but I believe these things happen to wake us up!"

Another time, Cindy was hand modelling at Old Street, she found herself standing on a ladder that was half falling apart, being made to twist and contort her body in all ways to get the shot. As a dancer, she was naturally able to hold a pose, but the truth was that it can only be done for so long. Holding her body away from the ladder and twisting her arm to reveal something on the tiles below her elbow became tougher than a game of Twister, and the director wasn't happy. While Cindy would never consider walking out on the job, after he continued to say, *"Move more"* and got angrier and angrier, while Cindy got more and more stressed. She stepped off the ladder and offered him a challenge, *"Well you show me how to do it then!"*

It must have been the first time he'd been talked to like that, but as he got up to prove a point, the director found himself unable to complete even an eighth of the movement and was much more accommodating to Cindy after that.

Bookings then began to get complicated. Showing up with an expectation of acting, Cindy might only be required to complete hand modelling as one was paid much more than the other. She very quickly had to know when she was being exploited. One such advert for an arts and crafts programme was booked for a hand modelling job but when the advert appeared on screen you could see Cindy's whole arms and face. It wasn't what she expected but with a pay cheque of around £5,000 for half a day's work, Cindy felt like she had lucked out. Still, she was keen to confirm exactly what the job was for each future booking. Terminology and clear communication became incredibly important, especially when combatting Cindy's dyslexia. Another source of income came from voice-over work, and while she found it hard to read the script at first, Cindy's voice was used for ads using different languages all over the world, included Batchelors Soup, that needed a Received Pronunciation (RP) speaker.

A Love of Hats

And it wasn't only hand modelling that Cindy took to; hat modelling was another calling. After a chance meeting with milliner David Shilling at a party, the pair went on to have lots of fun together with Cindy happy to display David's work on her head during the racing at Ascot. These dramatic creations meant that Cindy always ended up in the newspapers. For several years she wore his designs – often bigger and brighter than the year before, with stripes, bunches of flowers and lips all making an appearance.

Later, she offered to video a fashion show for David, which took place at the Hyde Park Hotel in front of 500 people. Cindy loved the excitement of organising the event with these beautiful models and in return was treated lavishly with food and drink, mingling with both the press and celebrities. It was a real lesson in marketing to her, understanding the significance of the people invited, from Lords and Ladies to A-listers, and watching how the next day, the event appeared in most of the national press.

Eventually Cindy decided to custom-make her own hat using Phillip Sommerville, a one-time milliner for the Queen.

This time, Cindy made the front page with her yellow gerbera design that was much brighter than anything she had worn before. For Cindy, this was a great opportunity but the practicalities of wearing such a creation were not always considered – on a hot, boiling day in the Royal enclosure, where Cindy had been going since she was 12, the yellow gerbera hat that matched her Moschino orange shirt suit began attracting green flies, and so hot and covered in splashes of Pimms and green flies, Cindy took home a different memory of that day. Yet in her study, there lies an album of press cuttings, and luckily, with the image taken in the morning, there she is on the front page looking as cool as a cucumber – not a green fly to be seen!

Still, David and Cindy remained friends and she remembers one unforgettable night over dinner at his townhouse. While appearing as his sidekick, Cindy couldn't help feeling that the atmosphere was rather strained. His other friends were Russian but didn't seem to want to join in with the conversation. She dared risk a joke to break the ice saying, *"You know we have a saying here in England, the grass is greener on the other side. I bet in Russia…"* As she paused, David was looking at her confused wondering what she was going to say, dramatically Cindy continued, *"I bet you say the snow is whiter"*. While David's jaw dropped and he sat there, mouth agape, a peal of laughter rang out from his friends and the evening continued, the mood much lightened.

The night could have ended in tragedy though as when Cindy ventured upstairs to visit the powder room and smelled smoke, once she pushed open the door she immediately spotted a baby's crib and to her horror saw that someone had left a lit cigarette that had accidentally dropped on to a pouffe. Luckily, she noticed in time before the damage turned from a piece of smouldered fabric to a raging fire and David was incredibly grateful to her.

Still, the pair did butt heads several times. When Chrissy Hynde of the Pretenders dropped into David's shop on Chiltern Street while Cindy was there, she got the impression that he didn't like her chatting to rock royalty as normally as talking to a friend. There was also another time when Cindy was trying to shoot her own reel to send to TV stations, looking for a role as a presenter, and when asked if she could film in his shop, David let Cindy down on the morning of the shoot. Luckily her friend Ruth Kaye and husband John Kaye had a wonderful shop called Ebony on South Molton Street. The day before filming, the pair said Cindy could use the shop – which was useful as not only were the Dream Boys booked to turn up, but also John Smith the footballer. The reel actually led to a job for Cindy on TV, but she felt it was the wrong role for her and turned it down.

Becoming a Serious Actress

While grateful for the opportunities that both working in the chocolate shop and the various modelling jobs provided, these were still only a stopgap for Cindy, who had remembered one of the lessons of Corona: to ensure you always had a valid Equity card. As a child actor, she had to work extra hard to gain membership to the union due to the restrictions on younger members, but now over the age of eighteen, there were several hoops to jump through to retain it.

A year later Cindy got there, and after six auditions, she landed the lead part for a film that was to be set in Georgia, Russia. Excited and nervous that she would finally be able to achieve something she had worked so hard for, it was now the union that pulled the plug on Cindy's dream. With tensions across the globe as they were, filming in Russia with pay expectations below standard was something they just wouldn't sanction. It left Cindy feeling totally disillusioned with showbiz. She had worked so hard to achieve something but lacked support from the union to see it through.

CHAPTER 2

GETTING NOTICED: THE BLUE VASE

The Car Crash That Nearly Ended It All

The next few years for Cindy were a whirlwind of excitement, opportunity, grief and an introduction to the world of art. But it almost never happened, thanks to a rather dramatic car crash outside St John's Wood underground station which could have killed eighteen-year-old Cindy.

It all started with a little bit of sibling rivalry. Cindy and her elder sister, Tracy, had never been close, something Cindy believes started the day she was brought home from the hospital. That first initial meeting of a squalling baby who would now be the focus of everyone else in the house, created an energy that has remained between the two ever since, although Cindy knows deep down that Tracy loves her – they are complete opposites, not just in looks but in attitude. Still, they both have a love and respect for their parents and family, which means that the two get together quite often and Cindy simply adores her nephews.

On this fateful occasion, a sizzling ball of energy inside Bryanston Court, excited to be going to play snooker in a pub with her friends, Cindy grabbed the keys to the Mini Cooper she had just started sharing with her sensible older sister. By that point, despite Tracy being in university, the pair were constantly arguing and Cindy remembers that during one fight, she was dramatically shut out onto the ledge outside, six floors above the ground level which was extremely frightening for Cindy.

This day, like most days, started with an argument: whether Cindy could leave Cookie, her beloved Yorkshire terrier, at home that evening. Despite living nearby Tracy often popped in to see Jill – and so Cindy grabbed the opportunity to take the car and meet some friends but then Tracy started an argument over Cindy's joy of running across the city to meet new people – who would look after the dog? Cindy knew that with Cookie by her side, despite being small and well-behaved, she couldn't relax and play pool if the little dog came to the pub that night. Eventually it was agreed that Cookie should stay, and as Cindy rushed to get out of the apartment and cease the argument, her eye caught the outline of her brown, bulky Filofax. Instinctively, she grabbed it.

Having just passed her test with 'clunk, click' drilled into her, Cindy began driving from Marble Arch in the dazzling light of the late summer sun. As she got closer to the tube station for St. John's Wood, a policeman was outside, directing traffic. Cindy patiently waited for her turn, now in no hurry, but as she went to cross, her car was hit, dramatically pushed on its side towards the station by a speeding driver. Cindy remembers a blinding light, and before she knew it, she was in an ambulance with smelling salts under her nose on the way to the hospital.

The Filofax in her green bag had mercifully not been damaged by the impact of the car travelling an estimated eighty miles per hour from the other direction. Still on the front seat, it contained the names and telephone numbers of her parents, which allowed the emergency services to get in contact quickly, meaning they could all meet at the hospital straight away. Luckily, Cindy was wearing her seatbelt, and although incredibly cold and chilly for a while as she went into shock after a huge bang to the head, Cindy quickly made a full recovery – albeit she missed her commercial shoot the following day.

As Jill rushed to her bedside in hospital as the medics checked her over, Cindy remembers her mother – while still in shock herself – cracking the joke, *"Thank God you're wearing clean, matching underwear!"*

While lucky to be alive, the news was less good for her beloved Mini Cooper. Not only was the other driver never found, but the road report went missing and a mix-up with her father's broker meant that young Cindy's name had never been added to the insurance, and with the speeding driver missing, it was Tracy – the named owner of the car – that was to earn both points on her license and a fine, something else for the pair to argue about. Her father, stoic as ever, simply said, *"Thank God, you didn't lose an eye, God forbid or something. Get over it."* Ever the actress, what Cindy found most upsetting was that she was unable to film an advert she had been booked for the next day.

While the relationship between the two of them has improved over the years, Cindy found a deeper friendship with older brother Craig. Despite Craig living with her father after her parent's divorce, and Cindy and Tracy living with their mother, Craig and Cindy have managed to stay close. Cindy calls him her 'Guardian Angel'; he's an absolute sweetheart to her and has always manifested as the 'strong big brother'.

She remembers a noisy house growing up, and in recent years, painting has become a therapy to help process the noise and angst of sibling clashes amongst her parents' struggles. She calls it 'the madness of life'. Each time she picks up a paintbrush, she goes into her own calm and colourful world until the bare canvas is complete.

Despite self-consciously running away from painting at school, she was still a keen admirer of the arts and in particular, artist Beryl Cook. Indeed, Cindy's own art has continued to be compared with Cook's throughout the art world. Like Cindy, Cook had no formal training but instead, a willingness to paint directly from the heart. There have also been comparisons with Jack Vettriano, another untrained painter whose images have found iconic status.

Drawn to the bright colours Cook used and the sizzling energy of her portraits, it was at this stage that young Cindy's life began to change as she became aware of her fascination with colour. Before long, she would go from working in a flower shop, living at home – occasionally booking modelling jobs and trying to make it as an actress – to becoming a wife, mother and serious artist.

Meeting the Love of Her Life, Roger

While the car accident has always been a defining life moment for Cindy, an incident once again with a vehicle was to bring her better luck: her husband Roger Lass, who she almost ran over when they first met in 1988. Cindy is somewhat of a typical Gemini, and Roger freely admits that living with her is like living with ten different women sometimes!

On one occasion, Cindy remembers sitting down to dinner with his extended family and talking about her Beryl Cook paintings. Roger's dad jokingly made a bet that if she was still painting in twenty-five years, he'd owe her £50. The bet was finally up just a few years ago, and Cindy would have triumphantly made him hand his money over, but unfortunately, he had already died some years previously.

Both she and Roger have now been together for more than thirty years; Cindy believes that Roger is her soul mate, and not only that, the pair have a soul contract together.

They were married in 1992, on the 9th of April. Another auspicious day, it was a general election for the UK government, the first after the resignation of Margaret Thatcher. While John Major comfortably held his position of prime minister, it was a rather different day for Cindy. She was photographed at her local polling station in her wedding dress, casting her vote on the way to the synagogue to marry Roger. The image made page 3 of The Sun, with an added typo that Cindy had actually married Ashley Lass, Roger's father. This was something that tickled them both, although Cindy's mother-in-law was less than pleased.

Roger was originally a surveyor who went on to become a property developer. The pair started their relationship in a small mews house together in Pimlico just before their wedding. The couple then embarked on a series of moves where they would buy one house that needed refurbishing while renting another until the birth of their first child, Oliver (when they moved to St John's Wood, coincidentally near the tube station where she had her accident, to a house that was also the inspiration behind many of Cindy's paintings).

Married life for Cindy was much happier than in previous years, but she was still not content. Her purpose in life had not yet been made clear, and with husband Roger determined to upgrade each house when he could, Cindy still faced months of upheaval and frequent moves. Her one surviving comfort from her childhood home was her dog, Cookie. Cindy loved to take her for walks on Hampstead Heath where she would bump into friends and neighbours. Although most of the time she carried her in a Louis Vuitton handbag, long before celebrities such as Paris Hilton made the look famous. Almost two years later, in March 1994 on a grey day – Cookie ill with old age – she went to visit her mum, Jill.

Auditioning for *EastEnders*

In the weeks prior, Cindy had decided to take one last shot when it came to acting, approaching the soap opera *EastEnders* over a potential role. In a meeting with Julia Smith, the director and producer, Cindy's accent – more Hampstead than East End – raised an eyebrow. She asked the question, *"And where do you come from?"*

Showing a flash of Corona spirit, Cindy snapped back with, *"Well, my mummy's tummy, of course!"* That was it – the

Hampstead accent decided that Cindy might be 'too posh' for the job after all.

Cindy later found out that it was Michelle Collins who did get the job, only Julia had changed the name of the character slightly. She was now 'Cindy Beale'. Later in life, when Cindy caught up with Michelle through her celebrity art for charity, the two laughed about how the character's name originated, although according to her mum Jill, *EastEnders* had made her daughter's name common.

Being a Good Daughter

Cindy's mother had been living between two apartment blocks, one in St John's Wood with her new partner while also keeping on her place in Holland Park. Eventually the decision was made to move in together at Jill's and so Cindy, being the ever-dutiful daughter, helped her with the move.

Cindy believes that when you do a good deed, you should do it with a good heart. This means that there can be no strings attached, no bargains to be struck – if you offer help then help you should be without expecting anything in return. But in doing so, Cindy has found that eventually you will be rewarded for your altruism. Or as Cindy believes, "*the universe catches up with you*". And while it might not be later that day or even that year, being a good person comes with its own rewards.

Which is why when Jill's neighbour started chatting to Cindy between trips back and forth to move over belongings, she felt that she should stand and listen, despite her promise to help with the moving. She found out that the neighbour was a retired doctor who was also interested in painting himself.

During the move Jill stumbled across a useful frame that she gave to Cindy, a poster of the winged horse Pegasus. It was later to become intrinsic to Cindy's artistic story. On her way back to the house for a final time to pick it up, Cindy bumped into the doctor who let her know that if she needed a place to exhibit any of her work (at this point Cindy had only ever painted as a hobby), then the Friends of the Orangery at Holland Park held an annual exhibition where she might do quite well. He insisted on giving her the number before she left.

Luckily for her Cindy has a great habit of keeping business cards and diary events and scraps of paper such as this, because while exhibiting at the Orangery seemed like another world away, it wasn't long before this brave new world arrived.

Becoming an Artist

The morning that Cindy heard the news that her shot at acting in *Eastenders* was not to be, she slumped round to Jill's to help her unpack. Perhaps in need of something to brighten up her lounge, or using a mother's intuition that her daughter was feeling low and in need of a challenge, Jill suggested that now might be the best time to paint a new picture she could hang on the wall of her blue lounge.

At first, the technical aspects of painting made Cindy feel like this was once again another burden – after all, she had no materials in the house and even if she did, finding them would be a challenge. Still, a dutiful daughter who loved her mother, she left Holland Park that rainy day to head straight for a local WHSmith in Notting Hill Gate, where she bought a pad of paper and the watercolour paints needed to make a painting. Back home in an empty mews house in Pimlico, Cindy focused on picturing herself in Jill's lounge and it was then that it happened. Looking at the white piece of paper, suddenly Cindy found herself catapulted into the middle of it, full of energy with the knowledge of what needed to happen next. Her thoughts spun – the painting was to be rectangular, patterned and full of colour and light. It was this exact moment that she was able to let the spirit that guides her into her heart. She gave herself completely to that painting, and each painting since has been the same.

Initially, she wanted to paint the vase that held carnations in her mother's living room, but on second thought, the carnations by themselves looked rather bare. Not only that, but the vase was also yellow with black spots, and with her spirit guide, she knew this wasn't the right look for her painting. Instead, she turned it blue (Jill's favourite colour) and added sprigs of gypsophila within the flowers. This perfect version of reality has been Cindy's ethos ever since; as an artist, she wants to improve what she sees rather than simply record it. Thinking about that time, Cindy says:

> "I can honestly say I gave myself to that painting. Imagine the feeling when you give someone a hug and get a big hug back, but just for a moment, your heartstrings pull in case it doesn't happen again. That is how painting felt to me that day and how it has been ever since."

And so, while running errands, Cindy added another to her list: to get the painting framed. She would often pass what looked like a little shop doorway that was a framer on Ebury Street, and so, bringing along that old frame that previously held the Pegasus poster, Cindy set about getting it framed. Proud of her ingenuity on the heavy paper, she wanted to show Jill and more importantly, brighten up her new place.

Little did she know that, upon entering the small shop, she was setting herself on a different path. Up until now, Cindy had struggled with her own identity; was she a ballet dancer, actress, model or wife? Now, here was the chance to become an artist, but was Cindy ready to take it?

She marched in on a mission to help her mother – this was supposed to be a quick job for Cindy. Once the painting was hung she could get back to thinking about what would come next in life. Instead, she met a smiling, kindly, well-dressed woman with red hair – Barbara Grundy. With the picture rolled up under her arm, Cindy attempted to flatten it out on the counter. Gesturing to the old frame and explaining that she'd like to use them to hold the new vase artwork she smiled at Barbara, words as blunt as ever, *"You're not going to make much money out of me!"*

Giving Cindy her full attention, Barbara looked down and asked, *"Who painted this picture?"*

Flustered and red, immediately thinking that Barbara didn't like it, Cindy stuttered, *"Me."*

But Barbara's reaction was completely the opposite of what Cindy had imagined. She said, *"Oh, it is fabulous! You must continue to paint – you are hugely talented!"* This compliment was somewhat hard for Cindy to take; painting was a way out for her – a clear path through the noise of the building work at home and her frustration with life – she wasn't ready to admit that she was good at it too. She almost wanted to look behind her, to make sure that this conversation was really meant for her. As Cindy collected her thoughts, Barbara took her painting (only charging her for a new blue mount that matched the soft tones on the heavy paper) and asked her to come back for the finished frame in the morning. Cindy explains what happened the next day:

"I'd gone back to pick up the finished frame and I was excited to see Barbara again. She'd given me such a shock by noticing my work, but it gave me confidence, and I couldn't wait to see the finished result. Only, when I walked in, Barbara was waiting for me, not only with the Blue Vase but with three other empty frames. *'Do you fancy doing a picture in these?'* she asked me. She made sure to say it conversationally, but to me those words were weighted. It suddenly seemed like a lot of pressure, but it was a challenge I desperately wanted to rise to.

"My mind went blank. *'What should I paint?'* I asked. Barbara just smiled and said, gently, *'Take them and see what happens.'* I put the frames under my arm and headed back to my car, convincing myself that Barbara was possibly a little nutty by trusting me to do this, but so incredibly grateful for the opportunity."

Heading back home to the house with no proper front door or banister, suddenly she was excited. Here was the perfect opportunity to escape into the colour of art and create a little bit of calm in her busy home. And it wasn't just Cindy who appreciated a bit of peace and quiet, Cookie the dog did too. It took a few more weeks to finish all three paintings but Cindy was desperate for Barbara's feedback – the energy inside her was once again palpable; her future was becoming a little clearer, with something inside her head saying, *this is your path, your journey, don't stop!*

Once again, she returned to 59 Ebury Street, offering her collection of paintings for evaluation, a mixture of real-life vases and plants. There was no real perspective, she wasn't trained after all, but charmingly, the plants appeared to float on the paper. Most of all, Cindy had filled the paper with colour, and on first impression, the vivid artwork was striking. Barbara loved them. She offered to put them in an art show she had lined up the following week with ten other artists. Delighted but thinking nothing of it, an invitation later arrived in the post and Cindy popped in on the night with husband and was absolutely flabbergasted to see that a few doors down from the small picture framing shop, Barbara owned a large gallery. Looking back, had Cindy known her work was to be displayed in such an environment, she's now not sure she would have had the courage to follow through.

The world of an art show was a completely different place for the pair, away from the hustle and bustle of the building site of home. The walls were full of fantastic oil paintings that looked more like photographs of expensive wine bottles and ripe cheese than the colourful, childlike paintings that Cindy had offered. She left the event excited but nervous. Compared to the others on display, her work was markedly different. She began to doubt herself a little but later heard that, incredibly, all of her paintings had sold. Barbara encouraged her to keep painting but this time with acrylic paint, as Cindy's style was loose and quick – she needed a paint that could keep up.

Cindy continued her journey with Barbara, who was such a sweet lady and a real guide through those early days of art, explaining the different ways to use materials. For Barbara, Cindy was a presence full of energy that she wanted to be in the gallery more and more. Although Cindy popped in whenever she could, her life was busy – but the two really did get on very well together. Cindy says,

> "I was always happy to help as through her I met a lot of lovely artists and people. And I was also keen to return the favour.
>
> "One friend of mine was a woman called Andy who was struggling with life somewhat after the death of her husband. I helped her to join Barbara as a part-time assistant and before long, she met her next husband while in the gallery. I still don't quite understand how it works but this type of energy you get from art and colour really works for me, it's very rewarding and I find it absolutely fascinating."

With her background in Corona, Cindy was used to falling into one thing and then moving quickly onto something else. The students had to get up to speed fast which meant that now, Cindy was always ready to take on an opportunity. Although as Cindy believes, you make your own luck. She adds,

"Comparing myself to others in the gallery, their work seemed so lifelike, using oil on board. But mine were so obviously from another world, the colours vivid and bright.

"It was all trial and error; I knew nothing about the different techniques or how acrylic compares to watercolour. I'm also embarrassed to admit that I am woefully ignorant of the history of art."

Cindy's nickname is Mrs Malaprop because she always gets her words mixed up (a malapropism is when you use an incorrect word that has a similar sound, though is often nonsensical). And while her mother was a fan of not showing people your ignorance, Cindy believes that as you age, you either need to ask or learn yourself, which is what she continued to try to do.

Cindy remembers someone commenting on one of her early paintings, adding that it was *'reminiscent of impressionism'*, but she had no idea what that was and would forever mix it up with other Cindy-isms. Still, her family often understood what she meant. They spoke Cindy, after all.

A few months later, excited to show her father her artwork on another opening night (a painting of a picnic blanket, lots of red and white that really stood out amongst the other work displayed), she saw a man in a grey suit coming out of the gallery, carrying her work under his arm. It was a turning point for Cindy.

"I remember thinking he looked like a businessman carrying my very gregarious bright painting out and

I hadn't even met the guy! I just couldn't believe that it was just gone. It had literally been put on the wall and someone – who I didn't know – had come in and bought it. Amazing. What was terrific was that it was the first time I realised that my work would sell itself off the wall. And that was a revelation."

Cindy, who at first wasn't confident in the 'off the wall' technique, realised that it wasn't her chatty and vivacious self that had sold the painting, it had actually sold itself. She explains:

"Now I realise that the energy of my work would draw people in, but it's taken since 1994 to admit that."

CHAPTER 3

BECOMING AN ARTIST: CONINGSBY

Putting on a Show

If time on her own painting was Cindy's bit of serenity, then a gallery show was Cindy's dopamine hit. The nerves leading up to opening night, the excitement of who would show and what would sell, was an intensity she had never felt in her work before. And now she had experienced a gallery sale or two, she wanted more.

And while Cindy's style has evolved, she is proud of how they stood out from the crowd and would sell so easily, despite her worry that there was so much other quality around. But now she had the bug. She says:

> "At the gallery, I felt like a fish in water; I couldn't wait to paint again."

The question was: what would happen next? Barbara had been fantastic, but without stepping off on her own, painting would only ever be a hobby. Yet by chance, or by spirit, Cindy has a way of making her own luck.

Meeting Stan Smith

For those first four paintings, once they were finished she took a photograph, and in that first year, she carried them around in her purse like photos of her children. A few weeks later, still in 1994, Cindy set off to meet a friend, John Marriott the film critic, for lunch at a private club. Always early, Cindy rang the bell, hoping to be let in. It was an older man in an old-fashioned grey Macintosh coat who opened the door. She explained that she was a little early and the man invited her to sit and have a drink with him. With her parents' words of *'never judge a book by its cover'* ringing in her ears, she agreed. They sat in a quiet bar and began to chat, although Cindy had no idea who he was. He asked about the type of art that she painted, and out of her pockets, Cindy pulled out the pictures of her four most recent works, all vases, plant pots and flowers. The man complimented her freestyle, although Cindy was quick to tell him that she was untrained and had just started her journey in art.

In earnest, the man looked at Cindy and said, "*You have your own unique style, please, never go to art classes.*" After a while, Cindy realised that John would probably be looking for her and made her excuses to go to the dining room. The man said, "*Wait, I will sign a form for you to be a member.*" Still, with no real idea as to his status in the club, she was simply glad to be proposed and accepted gratefully. Later when she left, she realised that he was no other than celebrated artist Professor Stan Smith. And the club? That was the prestigious Chelsea Arts Club where Cindy has been a member ever since after the chairman himself, Stan Smith, invited her to join.

Cindy left that lunch with a new confidence – for her, Stan has always been an angel to guide her. There was a reason why she was there that day, not just to meet John but to join an amazing club which would later become such an important part of her life through the help and support from other artists. Cindy realised that Stan would be important and something inside her encouraged her to go with her intuition and listen to him. And now, she's incredibly thankful that she did.

A few years after he died, Cindy was in a bookshop when she came across a whole section dedicated to the man who wrote many books on how to be an artist, including *The Artist's Manual*. A celebrated lecturer at Central Saint Martins, part of the University of the Arts London, and here he was advising Cindy never to take an art class, despite having students queuing up to take his.

Education is something that Cindy has always been sensitive about, and without a guiding force such as Stan validating her work, Cindy believes that she might have thrown herself into learning more about the art world, and certainly its history. However, his kindly advice changed her life course and gave her confidence to continue in her work, something which she still struggles with from time to time, even to this day.

Cookie's Death

While life had taken such a turn since she was sat in her mother's apartment on a grey day in London and asked to paint something to cheer the place up, there was still a reason to be sad. The death of her beloved dog, Cookie. For almost sixteen years, she had been a part of Cindy's life throughout her late teens, early twenties, marriage and early painting career, so when she began to become ill, it was a very hard thing for Cindy to go through. Cookie started to suffer from a series of little strokes, so she needed a lot of care towards the end of her life.

Even in the midst of this new artistic adventure, the stress never quite went away. One day in early spring, on a walk through Regent's Park with mum Jill – Cookie was being carried by Cindy to save her poor legs – the pair spotted an incredibly colourful row of pansies. On a whim, Cindy put Cookie down among the white and purple pansies and took her photo, determined that this would be her next painting. Captured in the picture, there sat Cookie, happy, lolling pink tongue stuck out, delighted to be around the people that loved her and surrounded by bright, beautiful flowers.

Shortly afterwards, Cookie died. But Cindy felt it important to paint through her sadness and finish the painting, even though it took several weeks to do. She says:

"It was very, very hard to carry on as Cookie died in the middle of me completing the painting. But once I got into the thick texture of the paint, it was also therapeutic. I still miss her so much; she saw me through the transition from girl to woman."

The painting now hangs pride of place in her colourful kitchen and is something that Cindy would never sell because it is filled with grief, which makes it all the more a painting that Cindy loves, as it is a part of her.

In total, there are around five paintings that Cindy feels she could never sell, but what she likes most about her Cookie painting is the irony that in just a few years' time, she would be known as a celebrity 'pawtrait' artist for her work painting famous people's pooches.

Opportunity Knocks at the Tennis Club

Up until now, Cindy had thought of her work for Barbara Grundy and her meeting with Stan Smith as a journey for which she was just along for the ride. Painting gave her a way out from her life, whether it was dealing with a house turned upside down or grieving her companion of many years, Cookie. But there was also another hobby in her life – tennis.

Together with Roger, the pair had joined the private Paddington Tennis Club as both a hobby and, as she was constantly beset by building works in the early days, an escape from her chaotic home. As a left hander with a good, relaxed serve most right handers struggled with, Cindy was in demand. She truly loved it there, and found the people fabulous, from knowledgeable London cabbies to shy millionaires, it was a great eclectic group of people that gave Cindy so much energy to be around. She would often come across for one of chef Linda's magic egg and chips for the bargain price of ninety pence.

Not only was it also a place that Cindy felt at home, but other celebrities did also. From here she rubbed shoulders with novelist Martin Amis, and eventually became best friends with a rock star and his wife.

One morning on court Cindy found herself across the from the most good-natured, long-haired man she had ever met, Dave Murray. Later on Cindy would be told he was a guitarist in a rock band – *Iron Maiden*. It turned out that Cindy had already met his wife, Tamar, a successful businesswoman who confessed she had been watching Cindy on court from the balcony of her apartment. She sought her out to ask would Cindy be up for game or two? The answer was of course yes and Tamar became one of Cindy's first female friends that she felt a strong connection with. The pair had enormous love and respect for each other and still do. Once off-court Dave went to introduce the two of them but to his surprise, the pair were already firm friends. Both Dave and Tamar would come to support Cindy throughout her various gallery openings over the years and they are still a dearly loved couple to both Cindy and Roger. Cindy says,

"Tamar was a huge inspiration to me, so on top of her game, had her own property business, completely different to anyone I'd ever come across. Kind and gentle. I can still hear her on court shouting *'Go for it Cindy'* when I was getting ready for my first solo show. Her support meant so much to me. I still adore her to this day. She is just incredible."

Despite Cindy having no official training and was self-taught when it came to tennis, she soon found herself in the women's team. Known for her front, she did very well! Although, looking back, Cindy wonders if this was all channelled from above. Marching into Barbara's shop, a chance meeting with Stan Smith and now a tennis club that would propel her forward as both a player and an artist.

Cindy loved nothing more than heading to the club with a friend, where, after a hard game, they could relax with a drink in the club and have a chat, but it was also the place which put her in touch with two men who would change the course of her life.

Committing to Her First Gallery Show

One day at the tennis club in 1994, a young Cindy Lass was meeting her friend Viv Marshall. The pair decided to sit on the club lawn watching a match when the talk turned to an upcoming wedding. Viv was unsure what to get as a wedding present for some joint friends of theirs. In a strange coincidence, Cindy remembered she had photographs of the two paintings she had framed so far, the blue vase and sunset tulips, in her purse and got them out to show Viv. "*How much?*" she asked.

Cindy was put on the spot; pricing has always been something she struggled with. On the one hand, the acrylic and gouache paint on the paper she was using could be expensive, not to mention she had to price for her own time and ideas, but on the other hand, this was a friend, and Cindy didn't feel that she could ask for something above what they might be able to afford. She had an idea. "*This is one of my favourites so I will sell it to you for £80 but if you ever find yourself not needing it one day please let me buy it back,"* she offered. It was a deal (and the painting has since been bought back into Cindy's collection).

But this was a deal that had an audience, as behind the pair was a man called Andrew Coningsby, a businessman who had just opened his own gallery in Fitzrovia, after spending the last decade in artist promotion as part of the executive team at Debut Art. He asked if Cindy was an artist. A little embarrassed at realising that her negotiations had been overheard, Cindy added nonchalantly, *"Yeah, I've just started."*

He shot back with, *"Got any more?"* It was fate. A few days later, they met again. Hoping that, like with Barbara, she would leave the encounter with a few more paintings commissioned, the outcome was actually much more eventful. Once Cindy's existing stock had been photographed and Andrew said that he liked them, with his gallery rapidly approaching its debut, he wanted to commission another forty paintings for opening night. In shock, Cindy agreed and went home with his words, *'you can do this'* ringing in her ears. But she was soon brought back down to earth with a bump. The builders had covered her work in dust sheets as their own endeavours advanced. They had resorted to hiding frames under the sofa to stop them from getting trodden on. As a burgeoning property developer, Roger had budgeted project by project, but nowhere in his calculations did he see his wife becoming an artist. Cindy quickly had to learn for herself now that there was paint to buy and framing to arrange – no wonder she was stressed. The small kitchen provided hardly enough space for one painting, let alone forty. While supportive, in Roger's logical mind it simply wasn't the time to commit to an art show.

Despite having this amazing opportunity, Cindy's family could see the stress she was going through, something which quickly became serious as Cindy was admitted to hospital due to dehydration. Her desire to deliver was hampered by her environment, something she simply wasn't able to change. And the truth was that she had never finished ten paintings, let alone forty, so while she spun around, jumping from terrified one day to excited the next, the chatterbox in her brain that she now knows as depression was getting louder. In her head, she was still an eight-year-old dyslexic that couldn't read. On her down days she would convince herself that she had fallen into the situation accidentally, that real artists would have understood the timing needed to create such work and so would have said no. Instead, as an untrained artist, she had hurriedly said yes and now could very well spoil her own reputation before she got started by turning this opportunity down. Eventually, Cindy came to the soul-shattering realisation that right now, she couldn't pull this off.

With a heavy heart, she went back to see Andrew to tell him that she couldn't do it. In his office, under his cool glaze, he refused her defeat. "*Listen to me, you shook my hand and we made a deal*" he said. "*I love your work and I believe in you! Instead of one week of exhibiting you can have two.*" It was just the right amount of encouragement she needed. After a bit of extra time agreed for logistics and now with a twinkle in his eye, Andrew turned to Cindy and said, "*Why are you still standing in my office? Go home and paint!*" And that's exactly what she did. Cindy says,

"Through not knowing where I was going but trusting my intuition and what was in my heart, I felt a pull to do my first show – even though I didn't really know how I was going to pull it off. In that moment in Andrew's office, I realised I could do it all, I just had to start."

Making a Friend for Life

On her breaks from painting, Cindy returned to the tennis club. As a good-looking, nubile twenty-something, Cindy was looking for directions to the reception one day when she asked a man for help and they started chatting. His name was Larry Adler, a famous mouth organ player. After ten minutes of chit-chat, he joked that she would owe him money for talking to her. Quick as anything, Cindy shot back, tongue in cheek, with "*No, I think you owe me money for entertaining you with my chic white tennis skirt and long bronzed legs!*"

They both collapsed into fits of laughter and just clicked, quickly deciding that they would become great friends. He promised to come to Cindy's debut and as the time got nearer Cindy felt nervous, despite not really knowing who he was, she felt that he would be a good judge. She invited him home one day to look at her progress and he broke the tension immediately on arrival, "*Don't you owe me money?*" Cindy quipped back, "*Look at the state of you I think it's you who owes me money.*" The pair giggled and went to look at where Cindy's work had been piled up in the bedroom, safe from the builders. Luckily for Cindy he loved it and said, "*The colours are vivacious – just like you Cindy.*" Downstairs he added, "*You don't know me very well but if I didn't like it, I'd tell you.*"

There was a significant age gap – Cindy was only in her late twenties whereas Larry was eighty, but the friendship continued, and for the next seven years until his death, the pair were unstoppable. Cindy got to know Larry as a truth teller, somebody who stood for integrity and with whom she could never move the goalposts, something she has greatly admired him for. He would joke with Roger, "*If I had a wife like this I would never let her out.*" And while Roger was happy to have such a friend in Cindy's life, Jill was a bit more suspicious. She didn't quite understand the friendship, especially why Cindy was so taken with him. But a few months later, she caught Larry on a TV show talking about the Second World War. He had wanted Cindy to go with him to the green room, but she was busy painting. Larry had the presenter in tears over his recollections and the suffering he had experienced in his home country. Jill later apologised to Cindy. "*I'm sorry I questioned why you were friends,*" she added.

An American by birth, Larry was an incredibly successful musician both in the States and across Europe, touring throughout the 1930s. However, during the McCarthy era in the '40s, like many famous Americans, he was accused of being a communist. He refused to cooperate with the investigation and was then blacklisted, barred from studios and found it hard to find work like many of his Hollywood colleagues. It meant that in the early '50s, Larry moved to the UK and lived in London for the rest of his life.

It was this experience that led him to be so open and honest with Cindy. He told her of some of the issues he had been through, including stories of fellow entertainers who had fallen foul of the same rules – such as British actor Charlie

Chaplin who had lived in the States for more than thirty years. His edict remained to always paint for herself and not others. Later in her career, after begging her to do a portrait of him (Cindy isn't comfortable with portrait painting – she would much prefer to paint a dog than a human face), she gave in and painted him on a lively background with a half-smile on his face. When the painting later sold at a gallery, he was angry that it had gone to someone else with no connection to either of them and so Cindy had to go back to the gallery and negotiate with the customer, promising a different painting, to ensure the portrait went back to her.

Larry would invite Cindy to the most lavish of parties where he would hold court amongst the guests and play alongside other musicians but if it was demanded he perform or 'sing for his supper', then this would upset Larry. One time he even asked Cindy to take him home immediately. Asking a musician to demonstrate a talent without prior invitation was the height of rudeness for Larry, yet he would never be far away from his harmonica, just in case he felt in the mood to play – party or no party.

Never one to mince his words and, even amongst the crème de la crème of the London scene, when asked for his opinion, he never sugar-coated it. Cindy loved him for speaking the truth. He died just as she started her charity work for Battersea Dogs Home on which he said, "*I know you're doing it for charity but please, paint what you want to paint.*" He went on to send her a poem which Cindy framed and still hangs in her home today. It humorously paints the picture of Cindy's rise to fame, through the eyes of a cheeky friend and confidante.

Cindy Lass, Cindy Lass
I've said it before, you're a pain in the ass
Your paintings are happy, they fill me with glee
But I don't like you being more famous than me
I'm well-known in Thailand, I'm famous in Siam
But in England you're getting more famous than I am
One great female painter is Rosa Bonheur
But now you're getting more famous than her
So Cindy Lass, Cindy Lass
You're a pain in the ass, you're a snake in the grass
But I love you to bits cos you've very nice tits
But you'll have to give up with this publicity blitz
So I leave you with this, my adorable Cindy
The blast from your fame's getting too goddamn windy

Across her extraordinary friendship with Larry where she was lucky enough to have dinner with him at some of London's most amazing restaurants, one of Cindy's favourite memories is remembering the night she sat as his wing man at Peter Stringfellow's naughty lap dancing nightclub, Stringfellows. Knowing they both had a wonderful, and platonic connection, Roger was fine letting the pair out on the town. Cindy says,

"I knew it was a special thing, Larry taking me for dinner. And we spent so much time talking about his past and regrets. But it was only when he died I realised how his management had taken a lot of royalties from him and it made me question who these agents are. It's something I'm passionate to tell young artists – just like he did for me, you always

63

need to have someone looking out for you as it's so easy to get taken advantage of.

"But the best thing about Larry was how he was so passionate about me being passionate about painting. He didn't see me as a wife, mother or daughter, he just saw me as Cindy. And everyone should have somebody like that in their lives to push them along. I know he wouldn't have always agreed with me doing my animal charity work, he liked my flowers and still life after all. But he was a wonderful man. I still miss him."

The Fabulous Barbara Windsor

After Cindy's chat with Andrew Coningsby she had returned home reinvigorated (somebody believed in her!), and grabbed her paints. Fast forward four months later and the finished forty paintings debut at the Coningsby Gallery alongside none other than one of the stars of the *Carry On* series herself, Barbara Windsor, who was shortly to take up her next role as the indomitable pub landlady, Peggy Mitchell on BBC hit soap, *EastEnders*.

As always, there was a story behind how the two of them hit it off, and it all started back at that unassuming nail salon, Supernail in Crawford Street, which seemed to be a beacon for the well-known ladies in the area. One day Cindy got chatting to someone who had such an infectious laugh there was no mistaking her, Barbara Windsor. Over time the two would sit and chat while having their treatments and became very comfortable in each other's company. She was like an

Aunty Bab's and because of this, Cindy would never feel comfortable asking for such a favour as opening her show, despite Barbara often asking in passing if she could help. However, help was at hand through Richard the receptionist; he had heard Barbara's kind offer and mentioned that his husband, Barry Burnett, was her manager. Would Cindy like him to put in a word?

Cindy knew then that it must be fate if she was being presented with the same amazing opportunity not once but twice and jumped at his offer. And that was how the East End Queen herself came down to support Cindy at the Sunday afternoon premiere on the 19th November 1995 at the Coningsby Gallery to open the show. She explains:

"Having Barbara open the show was so special. There I was, absolutely petrified about the big day, but she did everything to calm my nerves and was just a pro in front of the crowd. Part of me loved that it was all on show, part of me was petrified. But I think that's normal as it was my first major art show. We were all very fortunate, and I have Barbara, a wonderful down-to-earth lady, to thank."

Netty Spiegel

Still, the night before Cindy's debut show, she almost felt like not turning up as she was so incredibly nervous. Luckily, a phone call from a special friend managed to calm her down. Through her in-laws, Cindy had made friends with Netty Spiegel, a lady who she greatly admired after she escaped Nazi

Germany on the Kinder transport after her whole family was wiped out. At this point, she was a top designer, but Cindy knew her as a personal friend who was very special to her. The night before her gallery opening, she rang to ask Cindy how she was.

Together with Roger, the pair had moved into their new house in St John's Wood, and with Roger at it upstairs, Cindy felt she could be honest with Netty.

"I told her I was frightened. I was at a point where I had had lost control. There was no way to pre-sell anything and it was a very insecure feeling. And Netty gave me just the best advice. She said, '*Cindy, you're a great girl and a great artist; I love your use of colours. You've just got to go in there determined to have a good afternoon and think of the opening as a party. If nothing sells? Don't care about it. Just go to sleep, wake up, take a nice walk around the block and go to the gallery thinking it's like any other party.*'

"That ability to see a gallery opening as a party is something that has stuck with me. I've been doing parties since I was little, and I'm never phased about walking into a room full of people. Immediately, I went to sleep and was out like a light. The next afternoon, I needn't have worried; I walked in determined to enjoy myself and that was exactly what happened – it was a great event. Everything sold over the next few weeks and the opening was packed, a huge success, although that was just a bonus, the icing on the cake. But I'll never forget Netty's advice."

While Cindy was desperate to hold a few things back to remember the efforts she had gone through over the past few months, surprising not only herself but her family as well, Andrew the owner refused to let her 'sticker' anything. If an item appears with a sticker, it means that it has already been promised to someone else. This can be quite common for artists who want to keep a proportion of a gallery exhibition to keep or sell on later elsewhere. But Andrew was so impressed by Cindy's collection that he wouldn't let her hold back a single item. And over the next few weeks Cindy would receive a phone call or pop in every few days to chat with him and hear the news that more items had sold until eventually, there was nothing left. Cindy's show had been a roaring success. She was now officially an artist with a sold-out show.

A Whirlwind of Exhibitions Begins

But it wasn't just Cindy's famous friends that helped with gallery publicity. Cindy believes in fate, and while also working on her pieces for the Coningsby Gallery, Cindy remembered Jill's old neighbour's advice about the Orangery at Holland Park.

It was a great tip for her, she followed it up immediately and eventually submitted two paintings that would be shown – the first a painting of flowers in watercolour and gouache on paper, the other a loose figure of eight in acrylic paint on paper.

Cindy invited ten friends, all with different backgrounds and from various walks of life, and when the night came along they all somehow picked Cindy's work out from the other fifty or so artist submissions. There was just something different about the way she worked, whether it was how vibrant the colours were or how the paintings radiated life and energy. You could never pass a Cindy Lass painting and not know you were in her company. To her delight, both the paintings at Holland Park Orangery sold, and suddenly Cindy's confidence grew wings. She found herself accepting all kinds of invitations, including a one-woman show back at the Orangery in the corner of the gallery and has since never looked back. Cindy says,

"Yes, it's quite nerve-wracking getting up on stage, but the moment comes and goes. As for painting itself, well, I can only paint when I'm in the mood. Usually if I'm highly excited or coming down.

"I was amazed that while I felt I knew nothing it was clear that I was on the right path. If someone had told me that if I just picked up a paint brush and worked at it, I would have run away like a scared little mouse with a cat after me. But each step I've built up my confidence, little by little. Perhaps I've just been feeling my way through life but I was never scared of it – yet I am truly fascinated by marketing as even though I don't fully appreciate the principles, something inside me seemed to grasp the basics. And here I am."

The Deal with the Halcyon

Before Cindy knew it, she had had a sold-out show at the Coningsby Gallery, critically acclaimed praise for her debut at the Holland Park Orangery, and now another offer she couldn't resist. To showcase her art in the one of the hottest hotels in London, the Halcyon hotel – also located in Holland Park. After opening its doors in the early 1990s, it quickly established itself as one of the capital's most exclusive – and discreet – celebrity bolt holes.

Regarded as one of the city's best-kept secrets, the forty-four room hotel played host to an extraordinary amount of celebrity shenanigans in its short history before closing in 2002. It also featured as Simon Templar's London hotel in the Hollywood movie *The Saint*. It played host to some of London's hottest celebs and their entourage. Mick Jagger, Paula Yates, Liam Gallagher, Patsy Kensit, Liza Minnelli, Geri Halliwell, Monica Lewinsky, Robert de Niro, John Cleese, Naomi Campbell and Yoko Ono have all walked the halls and a party by rock band Oasis in one of the suites became the cover image for the single, *Cigarettes and Alcohol*.

Not only was Cindy's art on display (and on sale) but in return, the Lass family were invited to certain events and private dining opportunities when available. Cindy remembers,

"The Halcyon hotel in Holland Park was fabulous – that place was rocking. Downstairs, all the media would be there, alongside celebrities, and I mean real celebrities – Mick Jagger, Oasis and the like. It was amazing. I had around fifteen paintings on the wall for almost two years until they switched artists, but I had a great deal in that I would bring people in and pay for my drink but get the food for free. What a time!"

Despite the many celebrities she got to meet and greet in the Halcyon, her one defining experience is of moving her paintings in for the first time. With a garage fit to bursting with her designs, Cindy was let down on a van. After a number of renovations under her husband's belt, she was on first name terms with his crew – many of who are still loyal to him thirty years later. The team are not only treated with respect, they have become part of the family. And so, when Cindy was in desperate need of some help, at first she called on Paul Scott (Scotty) the foreman and then moved on to Paul the plumber (nicknamed Dillan) as he had the biggest van. She explains,

"At times, I realise my life must sound so glamorous, but when people think of me having fun with celebrities, I think of the hard slog it was to move all these paintings to the Halcyon in the first place. One day, I collared Paul from Roger's team. Making conversation, I asked, "*How do you train to become a plumber?*"

"Perhaps this was a bit obvious as he joked with me, "*No darling I didn't train, I just follow the pipes round.*" That was it, we became firm friends and together we hatched a plan to load the van up one morning at 7am to take the paintings from St John's Wood to the Halcyon. As usual, there was nowhere to park down Holland Park Avenue, and as I had paintings waiting to be hung, I was as high-strung as ever, desperate for my work to get shown in this fabulous place. Paul turned to me and said, "*You know what, darling, you need to chill out a bit; you've got to be strong for when something does happen – your life is good!"* It meant so much to me that he reminded me to enjoy it, and since then, life has been good but made ever sweeter by the people I've met along the way.

"Roger's builder Paul Scott, known as Scotty, ended up making the circles that I went on to display for Battersea and Celebrity Flowers. Each and every one of the crew has helped in a part of my tapestry of life. And lately, I've come to realise that every stitch in its fabric is important."

While Cindy has received support from many unexpected places over the years, she has always had the backing of family and friends. Even if they did try and warn her when she had bitten off more than she could chew. Still, it was a proud moment for Cindy when Roger's cousin, Michael Rosenfeld, finally saw her as an artist. He had a keen interest in art alongside his older brother Ian, an art collector. As he sat with clients eating in the hotel's restaurant, he was struck by the fact that he was surrounded by Cindy's work – he just couldn't get away!

Cindy recalls that he rang the next day.

"He was laughing, saying, '*I couldn't believe it, there I was in the Halcyon, in the restaurant downstairs, I look up and every painting has C.Lass on it – there was class everywhere!*' On opening night at the Coningsby gallery the photographer David Koppel pointed out that by signing my name C Lass it spelt class – which really delighted me."

Motherhood and Art Collide

From then on, opportunities in the art world continued to come Cindy's way and she began to get involved with charitable causes. But while her work as an artist was becoming more regular, there were about to be some big changes in her personal life. Cindy was pregnant with her first child and another move was on the cards. This time, to prepare for their larger family, the pair were moving into a larger house but it needed work, and so while the renovating was taking place, Cindy found herself renting in Abbey Road (famous for its connection with the Beatles) with a small garden for their dog, Ralph, once again surrounded by chaos. So, naturally, she decided to take on a project.

At this point, Anna-Mei Chadwick, a renowned gallerist, was also looking for her next exhibitionist for a solo show. She had seen Cindy's work and invited her to apply. So, armed with her portfolio, Cindy presented her previous achievements and the pair agreed that they would work together. Cindy describes Anna-Mei as:

"Tough, but a good tough who brings out the best in you".

Unlike the Coningsby show where Cindy felt rushed in everything from the paintings to the framing, Cindy was now able to use everyday inspiration to paint for the Anna-Mei Chadwick show. If she saw a bench or a particular tree in blossom, she would take a photo and paint from the recollection. Although sometimes she veered off track slightly, changing colours, backgrounds or bringing in new items altogether to her paintings. Cindy adds:

> "Everything I painted went into that show. Anna-Mei had a great eye and loved each painting I created, she insisted that they all went in, and amazingly, they all sold. I think you can never look at your own work and judge it accurately. I needed her to tell me to frame everything."

While the working relationship was great for Cindy, the sheer amount of painting was once again taking its toll, this time for different reasons. Once again, her world was very busy, and her maternity was catching up. Cindy would be exhausted by 4pm each day, but she was determined to find a way to paint. She went on to devise many different techniques for getting the best out of her mornings.

Now living in her newly renovated townhouse in Ordnance Hill, Cindy brought her creative talents to the dining room which had no window. Instead, she painted her own view of a stunning landscape to look out upon. Row upon row of flowers in vases on a bright red windowsill opening to a stunning corn-flower blue sky ensconced in a cream, latticed-framed window. It was such a sunny painting that when the pair went on to sell the townhouse, the woman buying it refused to complete unless Cindy left the painting. Something that Cindy took as a huge compliment.

Still, doing things her own way wasn't always easy. Early on in her painting journey Roger had arrived home to find all of her photos and material spread across the kitchen table – Cindy was in the middle of painting a still life – he pointed out that she couldn't leave the table as it was if they were going to eat. To keep the momentum, Cindy snapped a photo and completed the rest of the painting from this aide memoir. It was only at the gallery opening that Cindy realised the writing on the book cover she had incorporated in the still life was back to front. Somehow the camera roll must have been put in the wrong way round. Dyslexic, Cindy had copied the image letter by letter, and with everyone else convinced the mistake was a piece of Lass originality, it took a hapless bystander to point out the obvious. But Cindy wouldn't have it any other way.

The urgency that Cindy feels when she needs to paint can lead to several new ideas. And as is the artist's prerogative, she then cherry picks the best that she sees, before replicating these stellar points on the page. Cindy explains,

"Let's say I'm drawn to a bird in a tree, I would either sketch that now or I would photograph it and perhaps put it in a different tree. But if it makes me want to paint it, then that's exactly what I'll find the time to do."

Finally, the work was complete, and at four months pregnant Cindy once again got in the van to drop the work off before heading back to the gallery for opening night a few days later. This time a new friend also came, Anita Dobson, another denizen of *EastEnders*, Anita played Angie Watts in the BBC soap for three years until 1988 and in 2000, she married lead guitarist Brian May of ultimate rock band, Queen. Cindy and Anita had bumped into each other at Supernail, and Anita has been a huge fan of Cindy's work ever since.

But there was one other person who would always lay claim to being Cindy's biggest fan, her mother, Jill. Cindy says,

"My mum was quick to show how proud she was of me, strutting like a peacock when she saw people admiring my work, cutting my press clippings, but it didn't bother me. Mum loved that I treated everyone the same.

"Sometimes I don't remember what happened last week, but I remember meeting a person. For me, that memory is trapped inside a bubble, and it's a lovely feeling. And when I find something that makes me paint, I feel the same. Painting has uncluttered my chatterbox brain to allow me to recognise those moments. Instead of simply taking a picture and sticking it into iCloud, ready to forget."

Just two months after her opening at Anna-Mei Chadwick's, Cindy exhibited at The Grosvenor House Hotel, now six months pregnant. Alongside Anita there would also be another celebrity there on opening night, Patricia Quinn, the actress famous for her portrayal as Magenta in the *Rocky Horror Picture Show*.

A few months later, Cindy had given birth to her first son, Oliver, but that didn't stop her plans to continue painting. Amazingly, just two weeks after he arrived in September 1997, she opened her next solo show at the Sydney House Hotel in Chelsea, another success that was featured in *OK!* the celeb spotting magazine. This time Cindy was graced with the presence of friends Larry Adler and Patricia Quinn, *Solaris* actress Natascha McElhone and Bond girl Marilyn

Leonard, famous for being eaten by a shark in the action-packed film, *The Spy Who Loved Me*. Cindy was doing well, enjoying life as both an artist and a mother, yet as the years went by, something was missing.

CHAPTER 4

WHERE IT BEGAN: BATTERSEA

Giving Back

In September 2000, Cindy gave birth to her second son, Jack. Once the melee of a newborn had settled down, Cindy decided she wanted to do something for charity. She was finally at a point in her life where she felt settled and, dare she admit it, lucky. And while any spare time with two young children was still a luxury, Cindy felt she had the energy to take on a project that would also benefit a charity. Something that had been instilled in her from a young age, where she would watch her mother come home from event after event. Cindy understood the good work people like Jill would bring to a charity, but wanted to make sure she concentrated her efforts on one to make a bigger effect.

There were a few near to her heart that she had supported over the years, but it was animals that Cindy felt an affinity too. With the death of Cookie, there was now a new dog in her life, Ralph. While Cindy was quickly head over heels with this pedigree miniature schnauzer puppy, he really belonged to Roger and so although part of her wished he could have been a rescue, she had to respect Roger's wishes.

Inspired by Cookie's death from years before and the desire to give her passion for painting a useful outlet rather than seeing it as a hobby or simply 'work' – which would undermine its importance in her life – Cindy decided to look into whether she could use her art to raise money for charity.

It was here that she realised Battersea Dogs Home might be a good fit. Back then, it was yet to benefit from any of the celebrity connections it currently enjoys, with talk show host Paul O'Grady and actress Amanda Holden as ambassadors. Today, it is named Battersea Dogs & Cats Home, and its previous chief executive Claire Horton, who served between 2010 and 2020, was appointed Commander of the Order of the British Empire (CBE) in the 2020 New Year Honours, credited as she is with turning its fortunes around, in part due to highlighting its connections to celebrities.

But before any of this, Cindy had an idea first. "*I'm going to paint celebrities' dogs to raise awareness, and you'll make money,*" she told them.

The senior members of the charity were sceptical. "*I don't think that will work,*" said Director General Duncan Green politely but nevertheless, *Celebrity Pawtraits* was about to begin.

Because of her strong conviction over rescuing animals, Cindy managed to convince Duncan that her art would help, although at that stage she still wasn't quite sure how.

Most of the people Cindy was friends with had pedigree dogs, so she knew she needed to make a big deal out of rescuing animals. She had an idea to paint on these large, round backgrounds, knowing that she would cheekily ask Roger's builders to make them into large, forty-inch circular canvases. She ended up roping in the foreman, Scotty, who's great potential was usually put to work in making roofs and fabulous buildings. Instead, Cindy nabbed him one day and put him to work. When Roger turned up and asked what he was doing with piles of MDF instead of the usual materials, Scotty simply shrugged and said *"I'm helping your wife out"* as though it was the most natural thing in the world. Resigned, Roger left him to it. To Cindy he'll always be a sweetheart.

Roger was always encouraging in his own way. Cindy remembers back then when he asked, slightly bemused that his builders had been side-lined, *"Why aren't they working on a job? Isn't it more important to build a house?"* But understanding her desire to help raise important funds for an animal charity, he was soon on board with the idea.

Cindy started approaching celebrities through their agents and personal assistants, asking if she could paint pawtraits of their dogs to be auctioned off to raise money for Battersea Dogs Home, the oldest animal rescue sanctuary in the country – first established in Holloway by Mary Tealby in 1860, before moving to Battersea in 1871. She approached numerous celebrities in London, mostly through flicking through copies of *OK* magazine and hunting down their PAs.

By the start of 2001, her work *Celebrity Pawtraits* was almost complete. Cindy had successfully approached a number of celebrities in Britain asking whether she could paint their dogs' portraits and auction them in aid of the

Battersea Dogs Home. Sir Elton John, George Michael, Trudie Styler and Ivana Trump were just a few of those who said yes. Cindy found the hardest thing was convincing celebrities that painting their dogs was a good idea. She said,

> "The first one I did was of Elton John's dogs, and I was really nervous, but afterwards, I got a call from David Furnish to say they loved it, and it all spiralled from there."

David is a Canadian filmmaker who was Elton's partner at the time, the pair later undertook a civil partnership in 2005 before marrying in 2014. Once she had the couple's approval, and to Cindy's surprise, she was suddenly managing to physically speak to people she never thought she would hear from, Trudie and Sting for example, so great was the desire of these famous people to help with her cause. But the life of a new mother was never easy, it simply wasn't practical to travel around the city meeting people and their pets. Instead, Cindy requested photographs to help her speed the work along. Within weeks, she had received many photos of pets from the celebrities she had reached out to.

And it was here that Cindy could put her amazing Rolodex into good use, not only did she have celebrities to track down and pooches to paint, but with her newfound knowledge of gallery openings, she needed a stunning venue to host the auction. At one point, Cindy was considering hosting the night at prestigious auction house Sotheby's, who loved what she was doing. But she realised that for the money to really flow, it had to be somewhere that incorporated drinks and a social atmosphere. Home House in Portman Square, West London, was the perfect venue for such an occasion. Which meant that all Cindy had to do was paint. Once she had the celebrities agreed of course.

Reaching Out to Sir Elton John

Sir Elton John is one of the most well-known celebrities who has rehomed pets from Battersea. Cindy knew that if she could just get him involved, everything would fall in to place. Luckily Cindy knew Katie Boyle, four-times host of the Eurovision Song Contest, who was a committee member of Battersea Dogs Home for more than twenty-five years before her death in 2018. She thought Cindy was doing something brilliant for the charity and gave her the intro she needed to write to him personally.

After Cindy sent him a letter describing her hopes of raising vital publicity and funds for the home and then later her portfolio, he replied with *"By all means go ahead, I'd love you to do it but I'd love to see it before it goes into the show to know if we want to buy it or not."* and was kind enough to send Cindy a photo of two of his dogs who had been rescued from the shelter. Elton would credit his first Battersea dog, Thomas, with helping him to overcome some personal difficulties when he first visited the kennel in 1990. In Garry Jenkins' book *A Home of Their Own: The Heart-Warming 150-Year History of Battersea Dogs Home*, Elton said,

"I love rescue dogs, especially as they seem to really know they've been rescued and love you for it. They give you so much back and it's great to be able to offer them a secure and permanent home."

Cindy made sure that her paintings of Elton's latest dogs, Joseph and Dennis, were the first to be completed. She really wasn't sure how long it would take as something like this can take anywhere between a month to two months. Even if Cindy completes a little line or a splash of colour, as an artist she is constantly over the top of her work. Cindy finds her best results happen when she puts down the brush and revisits it once it is dry. Otherwise, it becomes difficult to see the likeness. That little line or brush stroke could be the one that brings the dog to life.

Cindy knew that once Elton was on board the rest of the world would follow – and they did. Unfortunately, she couldn't deliver the painting in person, but the couple did arrange for it to be chauffeur-driven to Windsor, as a Special Delivery. Cindy is still made up from their delightful response. She recalls:

"I was probably most nervous of how Sir Elton John was going to react. It was a huge step for me, because I knew that if he didn't like what I had done, I would not be able to use the finished pawtrait in the auction. When I took a phone call from David Furnish to say that Elton loved it and that I had really captured the spirit of the two dogs, Joseph and Dennis, I was absolutely thrilled. I had put so much of my energy into it that it was already one of my favourites – and still is!"

Elton and David went on to buy the art, telling Battersea that they wanted to immediately pay the £5,000 which would go some way to help swelling the coffers in its aim of building a new wing for cats – something that was achieved shortly afterwards in 2002. At the time, Elton said of his dogs,

> "I chose Joseph, our collie cross, because I love mutts, and he is just the most loving animal I have ever owned. We took Dennis, the border terrier, with us to Battersea to meet Joseph and they seemed to get along. When we took Joseph home, Dennis wasn't too pleased, and he sulked for two weeks. Now they are best friends. They don't fight at all, except when Joseph gets a bit too boisterous and Dennis has to remind him who's boss."

Later that year Cindy was feeling generous and found herself in her studio drawn to painting bright red poppies. She just knew that it would be something that both Elton and David would love and so parcelled it up and sent it off to them. At the beginning of January 2002, she received a lovely note from Elton himself, thanking her for her kind gift. Cindy likes to think of Elton sitting down quietly after the hubbub of the holiday period and finding a pen and paper to thank her directly – she has still kept his card. In the days of quick emails and short voice notes, Cindy finds that she values the written word more than ever. It shows both thought and value, two things which should be cherished by all generations.

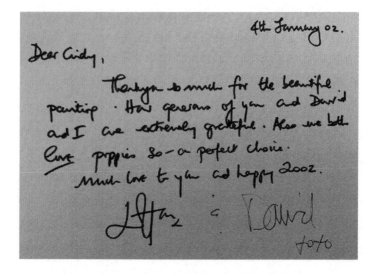

Dear Cindy,

4th January 02.

Thank you so much for the beautiful painting. How generous of you and David and I are extremely grateful. Also we both love puppies so - a perfect choice.

Much love to you and happy 2002.

Elton & David
xoxo

Now with Elton's seal of approval and the project in full swing, Cindy found herself getting up at 4am to paint so that she would have time in a morning before taking Oliver to school with Jack in the pram, and then going home to paint again before the afternoon school run. With many celebrities signing up to have their dogs' pawtraits painted, Cindy soon realised she needed PR and help to organise the *Celebrity Pawtraits* exhibition.

IAMS Sponsorship

By July 2001, she'd painted twenty-two pawtraits and was finally ready to exhibit them. A high-profile public viewing event was held at one of London's top private members clubs, Home House, where Cindy was helped by the fabulous Brian Clivaz. And while the majority of paintings had been bought by their famous owners, those that remained were available for the general public to purchase.

In the run-up to this hectic time, Cindy realised she needed to self-publicise more. With *Celebrity Pawtraits* her brainchild, it was only Cindy who was responsible for its success. Not only did she need press and sales on the night, she wanted the campaign to go much further. And for that, she needed a sponsor. Never one to throw away a business card, she remembered chatting to someone on the terrace of the Halcyon Hotel the year before who just might be able to help, Brian MacLaurin of MacLaurin Media. The only problem is that she knew exactly where she had put his business card – it was in one of the two bin bags of various business cards she had collected over the years. One afternoon, with only minutes to go before she was required on the school run, she began racing through the upturned bags on the kitchen table, eventually finding the one she was looking for at the bottom of the last bag.

Later that afternoon Cindy rang the number and, while Brian wasn't available, she found herself chatting to his business partner, Ian Monk, a previous senior editor for the *Daily Mail* and the *Daily Express*. Despite her lack of knowledge of PR, she explained her plan to Ian and how she needed some good PR to raise the awareness *Celebrity Pawtraits* deserved. As they brainstormed ideas – with a zero-budget complication thrown in for good measure – they came to the conclusion that the best way ahead was to continue with the idea of sponsorship. Ian warned Cindy that this would take time, but she remembers Ian as being very kind in keeping his fees down for the charity event, but her overall memory is of remaining terrified that the sponsorship would never appear.

Her fears were soon allayed. After making some initial enquiries, the dog food company IAMS immediately agreed to sponsor the *Celebrity Pawtrait* exhibition – not only did their ethos of helping dogs and cats live long, health lives through nutrition that makes a difference fit well with the event, but the team were also brilliant to work with. This was a massive relief to Cindy, Ian and all involved – a giant box on the to-do list ticked.

As the exhibition drew nearer, Cindy completed the pet pawtraits of celebrities such as Cate Blanchett's one-year old terrier Egg, Geri Halliwell's two-year old male Shih Tzu Harry and famous hat designer to the stars, milliner extraordinaire Philip Treacy's Mr Pig, a seven-year-old Jack Russell.

As the paintings were finished, Cindy started thinking about the event – what connections did she have to invite? In stepped her friend Bernie from Manic PR who was central to Cindy's excellent media relations skills. The pair had met a few weeks before her exhibition at the Coningsby gallery and Bernie was fabulously connected; two years earlier she had entered Cindy into the Cosmopolitan magazine and House of Fraser Women of Achievement Awards which were held at the Four Seasons Hotel in May, 1999.

That day Cindy sat alongside Tamara Mellon from Jimmy Choo and James Dyson, eventually losing out to Jo Verrent, now the senior producer for Unlimited – the world's largest commissions programme for disabled artists. The star prize was £5,000 but to Cindy the afternoon itself was priceless. She got to meet so many fantastic people and Bernie's connections continued to help her work flourish.

It was also Bernie who went on to introduce Cindy to art critic Robin Dutt who critiqued the show following Anna-

Mei Chadwick, held at the Grovesnor House Hotel in Park Lane, June 1997, just before Ollie was born. So when it came to needing someone to write the forward for Cindy's upcoming auction, she couldn't think of anyone better than Robin.

Finally, on the 1st July 2001 at Home House in London, Cindy launched almost thirty celebrity pawtraits to auction, and many still available for sale on the night. Robin Dutt's forward said,

> *Those who are familiar with the work of Cindy Lass may find this latest body of work a touch surprising. We are used to explosions of hot blooms, cascading vines and tufts of impertinent grass. Vases of Fauvist flowers are more her style. But dogs? Inspired by the work of Battersea Dogs Home, which has done sterling and very necessary work since 1860, Cindy came up with an idea to a address a very serious subject in whimsical and playfully ironic way. So here we are with Celebrity Pawtraits – images of the canine friends belonging to sparkling stars from all walks of entertainment.*
>
> *The result is a purposefully amusing and deliberately naive presentation of these varied pampered pooches in, of course, classical, Lass-ical settings of lush vegetation and day-glo flowers.*
>
> *Catch them in profile, frontal-friendly or half-turn contemplative. These telling studies are reminders of other less fortunate cousins who deserve just as much love and attention. Certainly paws for thought.*

Most of the celebrities had been generous enough to buy their own pooches – donating as much as £5,000 per painting, and making for a fabulous evening. Much to Cindy's delight, the art show was a huge success – her work raised close to an incredible £50,000, and she was supported on the day by celebrities such as Uri Geller and Michelle Collins, who Cindy had asked to open the show and was so generous with her time, bringing her mother and daughter along and giving an amazing speech. She also bought her pooch's pawtrait on the spot. But what Cindy was yet to appreciate was that *Celebrity Pawtraits for Battersea* was just the start. And in total over her career, her paintings of celebrities' dogs – both in London and New York for separate charity events – have raised a huge amount of money.

A full list of celebrities whose dogs Cindy painted for *Celebrity Pawtraits – Battersea Dogs Home:*

Cate Blanchett
Geri Halliwell
Sir Elton John
Normandie Keith
Phillip Treacy
Sir Richard Branson
Michelle Collins
Trudie Styler
Lady Victoria Hervey
Griff Rhys-Jones

Uri Geller
Sara Cox
Ivana Trump
Vanessa Mae
George Michael
Antony Worrall Thompson
Amanda Wakely
David Soul
Paolo Moschino
Chrissy Iley

After the event, Battersea Dogs Home was, inevitably, incredibly grateful for all the money and awareness that *Celebrity Pawtraits* had raised. "*Cindy's idea was fantastic, and the paintings looked great,*" said Duncan Green.

Cindy's number one supporter Jill was also quick to tell her how proud she was of her work, saying, "*You have put rescue dogs on the map!*" In recent years Battersea alumni have even found roles in the Government, with Palmerston and Larry the cat given titles of 'Chief Mouser of the Foreign & Commonwealth Office' and 'Chief Mouser to the Cabinet Office' respectively.

Although Cindy had held commercial exhibitions before, it was this event for Battersea that made her realise that charity work gave her the greatest pleasure. Cindy explains,

> "You really do get something back from organising an event such as this."

However, there is a reason for the saying 'never work with children or animals' as Cindy discovered on many occasions during that special time. It is, after all, quite a big ask to expect animals to pose for any length of time, and not all of her subjects wanted to stay still – even the most famous dogs wriggle, lick themselves or simply run off. She laughs:

> "That is something I have had to get used to. In the end, I often have to rely on photographs."

Working with Dogs

A case in point was, while completing her paintings for Battersea, Cindy met David Soul, aka Hutch from *Starsky and Hutch*, who had been doing great work highlighting the plight of Asia's dog meat market. He came to visit Cindy at her house with his girlfriend at the time, actress Alexa Hamilton plus his own pooch, Czechy, a five-year old male poodle. Only the dog couldn't sit still and went to play rough with Cindy's dog, Ralph. The scene looked like an episode straight from *The Benny Hill Show*, with the trio running around trying to catch the dogs. Eventually, the animals calmed down, and Cindy took photographs to work from instead.

Each painting took around two months to complete, but Cindy made the whole collection gloriously bright and cheerful. Cindy tends to work in watercolour and acrylic, producing an explosion of colour and vitality. Yet for her, it becomes so worth the hard work and dedication when she hears the positive responses from the pet owners.

George Michael

Wham! singer George Michael's pawtrait featured his old and faithful golden retriever labrador, Hippy, who passed away shortly after the painting was complete. It was a particular tricky painting for Cindy as it was a composition painting, including both Hippy and Mo, a previous puppy that George's PA revealed had tragically drowned outside his home in the River Thames. Working from around eight individual photographs, the painting that Cindy was able to put together of the two dogs was something George went on to treasure. He told Cindy that he absolutely loved the work and found great comfort from it. She says,

> "George was at home writing a lot and so I wanted to give him a bit of happiness through this composition

work of his dear dogs. I feel life is about energy, colour and love so I'm pleased he enjoyed it, although it was heartbreaking to hear of his own death in 2016.

"While most of the celebrities I worked with bought their own dog's portrait it's brilliant when someone like George Michael rings to say how thrilled he is that I have captured his dog's spirit. I just can't put a price on that feeling."

Cindy felt so touched by George's reaction to his dog pawtrait that when she went on to create Celebrity Flowers in 2006, she wanted to include a flower for him. The resulting *Sweet Wonders* was inspired by his favourite flower, the orchid. Cindy says of the work:

"Even in the dullest corner of a room, such a painting glows, transforming the space into a warm, vibrant atmosphere. Orchids are the sweet wonders of life, and I knew that they were his favourite flower. *Sweet Wonders* will always remind me of his gentle soul."

Sadly, the Wham! singer passed on Christmas Day in 2016. When it came to *Celebrity Pawtraits* Cindy believed that most people wanted to help not just for a good cause, but because of the burgeoning media interest in mental health and physical lifestyle choices. Dogs were seen to be part of the family nucleus with a whole luxury pet industry quickly establishing itself, something that still thrives to this day.

Cindy is reluctant to admit that she put dogs on the map – her ego simply wouldn't let her, although she is happy in the knowledge that she played a part. Although Jill was right to some extent, Cindy helped Battersea become the celebrity friendly rescue centre it is today. Her main aim all along had been to raise awareness and funds. Because of her *Celebrity Pawtraits* campaign, Battersea has been able to build a feline wing and no longer waits for charitable legacies. Today, they have HRH, The Duchess of Cornwall as their Patron, and many celebrity endorsements from the likes of Sir Elton John, Simon Cowell and Paul O'Grady. Cleary, whatever spirit that guided Cindy that day into helping, it seems to be still working.

One unnamed celebrity, rather harshly, informed her that they preferred another painting that had been done of their dog previously, which Cindy admits made her feel a little miffed after putting in so much work. Nevertheless, she acknowledges that her interpretation may not be to everyone's taste – art is so subjective, after all – and shrugs it off with ease.

Trudie and Sting

Actress and director Trudie Styler alongside husband Sting, the frontman of rock band *The Police*, told Cindy how much they loved their painting of Irish wolfhound Gideon.

The pair are well known for their own humanitarian work after starting the *Rainforest Foundation Fund*, dedicated to protecting rainforests and indigenous people, while Trudie has produced regular *Rock for the Rainforest* benefits at Carnegie Hall in New York.

When Cindy dropped off the pawtrait for Trudie and Sting at their Mayfair office, she was told that it would be going off on its travels on a private plane to be hung in their villa in Tuscany. She really does have her artwork everywhere.

Gavin Rossdale and Gwen Stefani

For Cindy, the best part of this new exercise was hearing everyone's reaction to her paintings. She would be sent messages of where the pawtraits would end up and everyone seemed to delight in finding the right place in their homes for Cindy's paintings, but sometimes it wasn't to be.

When Cindy was still searching for celebs to get involved in the *Battersea Celebrity Pawtraits*, Cindy bumped into Gavin Rossdale, the lead singer of band *Bush*, on Primrose Hill with his thirteen-year-old male Hungarian sheepdog, Winston. After the pair got chatting he agreed to take part, thinking that Cindy would only paint something small in black and white. Once the painting was finished, Cindy then went to drop it off at the house he shared with his fiancé, later wife, Gwen Stefani, lead singer of band *No Doubt*, who absolutely loved it.

There was only one problem; Gavin hadn't realised that Cindy painted in colour and on a large forty-inch circular canvas. At that point, the couple's London townhouse had a monochromatic colour scheme which simply wouldn't work. What's more, the art was much bigger than they had anticipated. But the pair soon found a solution: they suggested that instead of turning it down, it would be shipped across the pond to their pad in LA, which was a much better fit for the style.

While this would still support the charity, it was something that felt incredibly wrong to Cindy, even though this was for a charity and the money would be useful, she was a London artist – and so she just knew that it should stay in the UK.

Stood in their black and white kitchen mulling over the future of this new painting, Cindy countered back quickly with a suggestion of her own. At this point she had her own fan base of collectors and knew that it would get snapped up quickly. They were both happy to agree to this and subsequently a collector of Cindy's work went on to buy it the day of the auction.

Cate Blanchett

Australian actress Cate Blanchett – famed for her role as Queen Elizabeth I in the Michael Hirst film, *Elizabeth* – was determined to keep the painting Cindy created of her dog 'Egg' after it had been displayed in the Home House show. To her, Egg was as much her baby as any of her children and demanded reassurances that she would be able to have it back afterwards.

What many may not know is that Cate Blanchett was a friend of Cindy's before the exhibition was ever thought of, after the pair had met at the Film Choice Awards and started up a friendship. While in London for the post-war play *Plenty*, (where she played Susan) Cate came over for dinner to see Roger and Cindy.

It was a few nights before Cindy had her miscarriage and while tired and struggling in the early stages of pregnancy, the pair were delighted to host her for a late supper. She knew that Cate was excited to see baby Oliver, and as she leaned over the cot Cindy heard her say, "*I can't wait to have kids!*" Cate went on to have three boys and a daughter and has an amazing marriage with her husband, playwright and screenwriter, Andrew Upton. To Cindy she is a great lady and while they are currently oceans apart, there would certainly be big hugs and squeals in the street if the pair were to bump into each other again.

Uri Geller

There have been a number of pivotal spiritual moments in Cindy's life, some that affected her work and others her family life. But there was one celebrity in particular that seemed to set Cindy on a new path to self-discovery, Israeli hypnotist Uri Geller. He had originally sent her photographs of his three dogs, male greyhound Jon Jon, male chihuahua Chico and fifteen-year-old female dobermann, Medina. Cindy wasn't to know at the time but Uri later claimed that not only did his five-year-old dogs Jon Jon and Chico look like him but he found them both extremely intelligent and could even communicate with them telepathically.

The pair got to know each other better as Uri invited Cindy to his countryside mansion in Berkshire. He had just been visited by singer Michael Jackson and Rabbi Shmuley Boteach and the energy inside his home was like nothing Cindy had ever felt before. While she had always been receptive to people's energies, this was something completely different.

As she arrived, a classic American car sat outside the entrance where Uri showed Cindy how he could make forks stick to the engine. The car was covered in bended forks and spoons. Out ran the dogs that by now she knew so well, Jon Jon and Chico, to greet her and Uri explained to Cindy that the pair knew when he was ready to take them out. Amazingly they would never confuse walkies with any other times that Uri might be around.

Cindy isn't sure if it was seeing the open and honest way Uri explained about energy, vibrations and healing, but she was intrigued by his vast collection of crystals and the two talked for hours about the properties within. It would set Cindy on a path where she became much more in tune with her feelings, although she would learn not to question them, but instead to work with the emotions that would appear. Speaking on her time with him Cindy says,

"Uri Geller was charming, he loved my naïve style, that I was untrained and making awareness, ultimately raising money for Battersea Dogs Home."

That meeting with Uri was fascinating for Cindy, not just for his guidance in spirituality but also to see him clearly adored by a loving wife and family. For her, it was a real eye opener that he had managed to forge forward against others' disbelief. As Cindy went on to develop her own spirit, she believes that her trip to Uri's could have prompted certain parallels with her own life. But Cindy has always maintained that her abilities should never be exploited for monetary gain, which is a huge part as to why she has carried on with her charity work for so long.

Cindy left Uri's house determined to investigate the powers of crystals for herself. A decision which would turn out to be life-changing further down the line.

CHAPTER 5

AFTER 9/11: WORKING WITH DOGNY

Supporting New York Charity DOGNY after the Terror Attacks

Following Battersea's huge success, Cindy found many requests for help were thrown her way, but with a busy family life and a new purpose to only get involved with events she felt a deep connection too, there wasn't anything that took up her time as much as *Celebrity Pawtraits*. What Cindy would prefer to do was donate a painting to a charity, which could be sold at auction and raise money for good causes that way.

But suddenly, on September 11th, 2001, the world changed. Peace was under attack, and what Cindy later found out was that man's best friend was also among the many casualties listed that day. When DOGNY got in touch, Cindy gave it her full attention. She learned that DOGNY was a charity in New York set up after the attack on the twin towers of the World Trade Centre, to help raise awareness of the heroism of dog rescue missions that took place that day. It was initially founded to help the American Kennel Club (AKC) initially deliver an X-ray machine to Ground Zero to help rescue dogs that had been hurt in the search for survivors. But it became much more serious with dogs quickly becoming sick from inhaling smoke and dangerous jet fuels or burned from the rubble as they did their job. Many sadly perished shortly afterwards.

The AKC also donated much-needed medical equipment and covered all veterinary bills for dogs injured at Ground Zero. The fund was launched with DOGNY, America's Tribute to Search and Rescue (SAR) Dogs, a hugely successful public art initiative.

Like many of us, Cindy remembers where she was when she heard that America was under attack on September 11th, 2001. Together with Jill, the pair had attended a craft fair in Earl's Court and when they both emerged to catch a taxi home, Cindy remembers that it was so eerily quiet on the streets of London that you could hear a pin drop.

The taxi driver tried to explain that there had been an attack, but she couldn't quite comprehend the seriousness. It was only when she got back home to St John's Wood that it hit her, while the attack took place in the morning in New York, back in London this was the time just after the school run. With the nanny making fish and chips with the news on in the background, Cindy was convinced her small children would have seen everything. She spent the rest of the taxi ride back wondering what sort of questions would face her back at home, and how she had to tell her two smalls boys that there weren't always good people in the world. Cindy says,

"At that age it was very difficult to know what to discuss with them; Ollie had just turned four and had started primary school, while Jack was only one year old. I wasn't sure what they had seen so I just let them talk it through – on both that day and the months and years afterwards. It was a very weird time and I don't think the world has ever gone back to how it was before – a time of innocence really. 9/11 was the turning point."

While heartbroken at the sight of the carnage and devastation on our TV screens, what most failed to understand was that tragically, many serving dogs were lost in the attack. A high percentage of the few dogs that did make it out alive had inhaled toxic ash and were so badly burned they had to be put to sleep. Over in New York, the American Kennel Club sprang into action to honour and celebrate the estimated three hundred dog-handler teams that volunteered their time and their animals to help with the rescue mission. And so led by Dennis Sprung, DOGNY: *America's Tribute to Search and Rescue Dogs,* a fund-raising and public art project supported by the AKC was created.

The project's symbol would be a German Shepherd dog sculpted by artist Robert Braun and cast at the Meisner Gallery. The breed was selected because it is one of the most widely used in canine search and rescue, and there was one key dog in particular that the charity wanted to highlight. The lead dog at the time for the New York Police Department (NYPD) was a German Shepherd called Apollo, at almost ten years old he was a great worker – so much so that the other dogs and handlers followed Apollo's cues. When the call came to downgrade the operation from rescue to recovery, it took three large police officers to pull Apollo off what remained of the pile of rubble at Ground Zero. That old dog just wouldn't give up hope.

And so, a call was put out for artists to paint the 111 fibreglass sculptures – many emblazoned with patriotic colours, others celebrated by well-known sponsors such as the New York Yankee's or the cast of *Mamma Mia* on Broadway. These were then placed around the five boroughs of New York between August and November 2002, before being collected and auctioned off. Cindy was one of the artists who heard the call and was more than happy to travel to the U.S. to paint her own version of a dog of hope, contributing to the $3.5 million raised for search and rescue organisations by the charity.

Cindy agreed to fly out to New York, staying with a friend of hers, Penny Novick, where she painted on the larger-than-life fibreglass, a German shepherd in vivid greens covered with daisies, with a bright blue head to represent the 'Lassian sky'. It was here that photographer Mary Bloom, known as photographer to the Dog Stars, came to document Cindy's work, kindly sent by DOGNY. Cindy went on to stay in touch with Mary until her death in October 2021. The pair found that with a love of dogs and spirituality, they were both kindred spirits. These are the parts of life's journey that Cindy loves the most; meeting people, creating pieces that go on to be enjoyed or raise money – a cycle that is hugely cathartic for her.

In an interview with the American Kennel Club (AKC)'s copy editor, Bud Boccane, Cindy told him how she had painted the fibreglass German shepherd in mainly primary colours to appeal to children "*because the next generation is so important to the world*". With her vision to make people smile and spread positivity, Cindy used the simplicity of daisies to spread her message. She explained:

"Blue is subconsciously my trademark colour. I always love to use cobalt blue, and I love daisies – the pureness of the flower. But tellingly, having flown out to New York instead of being a native painter, I also didn't have that long a time to do it right. And I also had to get special paints – I never seem to have anything go smoothly!

"I managed to fly out during the kids' school term and somehow tell my brain to switch off from whether they had their backpacks and lunch money and focus instead on giving the paints over to myself and picturing a free, safe and celebrated animal. I hope that's what I've picked up, as I wanted to imagine the dog running free."

But that wasn't to be the end of Cindy and DOGNY. After hearing about the success of Battersea, the AKC asked Cindy if she would consider doing something similar over in the States with all benefits going to DOGNY. This was something Cindy knew she wanted to be a part of. A replay of *Celebrity Pawtraits*, with the charity this time as DOGNY. More celebs, more paintings, more dogs. Roger couldn't understand why she was putting herself through it all again, the flights to America, the painting and eventually the charity auction, but this cause was so close to her heart she couldn't say no. She started approaching celebrities and soon found that there was a real willingness to help 9/11 charities.

And so, two years after Battersea and still wanting to raise funds and help the charity, Cindy went on to hold a similar show, this time stateside for DOGNY. She painted the pets of Hollywood and the Big Apple's finest.

A full list of celebrities whose dogs Cindy painted for *Celebrity Pawtraits – DOGNY:*

Shirley Maclaine
Arnold Schwarzenegger
Dame Elizabeth Taylor
Alan Cummings
Cindy Adams
Heidi Klum
Karolina Kurkova
Sigourney Weaver
Chita Rivera
Mary Tyler Moore
Marty Richards

Casey Johnson
Kyle MacLachlan
Brad Pitt
The Osbournes
Kim Cattrall
Kirstin Davis
Sarah Jessica Parker
Jennifer Lopez
Kelsey Grammer
Billy Joel
President Bill Clinton

Chita Rivera

One of the first celebrities in the U.S. who was to benefit from Cindy's painting of her pooch for the DOGNY project was American actress, singer and dancer, Chita Rivera. At the time she was on Broadway in the musical show, *Nine,* and so immediately Cindy and Jill got tickets to go. After being in touch with her personal assistant for so long, Cindy received a very kind offer to meet Chita backstage, a request they simply couldn't say no to. Cindy explains:

"I didn't know who she was, but my mum said she was the first person to get the *Westside Story* lead part; as she absolutely oozed glamour and old Hollywood. We went to see the show – luckily, we had tickets for the first few rows which you needed to get up close with that amazing Tango. I thought it was so interesting, and she was just sex on legs. It was the most sensual thing I had ever seen, phenomenal!

"Prior to that, we had seen her two days before as she wanted to see the painting before the show, and I was lucky enough to snap a photo with her. She loved the painting so much she said she didn't want it to go in the show, telling me, *'I want to hang it in my bedroom now.'* And because she really was a legend, how could I say no? My mum was so thrilled, and it made me feel so happy to make her proud. Every time I think about that painting, it makes me think about those amazing times in New York. So many people wait for things to come to them, but I realise now that you've just got to make it happen."

After the big reveal of Casper, the Maltese terrier, Chita was thrilled. She mentioned that she had been instantly drawn to Cindy's painting, putting it in her bedroom without a second thought. Ultimately Cindy is tickled to know that such big stars have her work featured prominently across their houses, from kitchens and lounges to hallways and now – a bedroom!

Arnold Schwarzenegger

Cindy had planned to work with celebrities such as Arnold Schwarzenegger in person for her DOGNY portraits but, due to commitments at home (and a slight fear of flying after the sad events of 9/11), she decided to work from photos alone. But there was one image that stood out above all others. Here, Cindy explains:

"I was really excited to produce a painting for Arnold Schwarzenegger – Arnie – and he didn't disappoint! My boys loved him in our house and had watched all the *Terminator* films. I had wanted to meet him to see those muscles in person and had hoped to get over to the States for a private show, but the timings simply didn't work with young children at home. Still, he sent over a photo which made up for it and more!

"There he was in a tight vest on the hood of his Hummer, cuddling this little poodle at home in LA, with his two golden retrievers also in the frame. I thought it was sweet to see such a strong man cuddling up to a tiny dog with his muscles on show. It was brilliant to have it hanging in my office – such a talking point! When I finally did get the canvas over to him, he loved it because nobody seems to realise that I'm painting these massive circular canvases – they're so different to anything else. From the canvas itself to my style of painting."

Kristin Davis

With big celebrity names attached and Cindy's own fan base swelling, *Celebrity Pawtraits* is considered a success (together Battersea and DOGNY has raised a huge amount of money for charity) but there were some instances where things got lost in translation, especially when dealing with more than twenty celebrities and their personal assistants at the same time. The deal was that Cindy would send each finished pawtrait to the celebrity for their approval; this gave them the first chance to buy the piece before it went up for general sale. Only it didn't actually matter if the celebrity bought the item or not, Cindy still needed the pawtrait back to display on auction night for a limited time before returning or sending on to a new owner. It was a simple process where any items promised to celebrities would simply have a 'sold' sign prominently displayed, both in the auction catalogue and on the wall.

Kristin Davis (Charlotte in *Sex and the City*) never actually gave the painting back for the exhibition once it was dropped off for approval. Of course, the cheque for Kristin's Golden Retriever, Callie, soon appeared and Kristin even later waxed lyrical about the painting in a two-page article in the *New York Post*, where she described how happy she was to hang it in her apartment. Still, it was so bizarre that Cindy was quite puzzled about it at the time – but she laughs on it now, after all – the money went to charity and Kristin seemed to like Cindy's work, so a success all round. Cindy says,

"I loved Kristin Davis, she was the one I really liked in *Sex in the City* and her personal assistant was really charming. Sometimes people can misunderstand the process but overall, I was just happy the charity got the money. To me it was a mix-up that I can laugh about. I'm just glad to hear that my work is so popular with my favourite celebrities."

Charlie Sheen

With time flying by so fast sometimes, all Cindy has is a memory of a feeling to hold on to from such a time. For instance, she remembers that actor Charlie Sheen's French bulldog, Hank, loved eating pancakes. Luckily, she has whole albums full of press clippings and mementos from such brilliant occasions. Hank's pawtrait later became almost as well-known as her work for the Queen once Cindy teamed up with a certain major Italian food chain of restaurants for further charity work.

Heidi Klum

The German-American model was already involved with DOGNY with the initial fibreglass paintings and so was more than happy to let Cindy paint her two-year old Jack Russell, Shila. The pair would travel between Germany and America as Heidi divided her time between family and work, so the young pup was brought up on traditional snacks from both countries – although Heidi said that her favourite food was liverwurst – a type of liver sausage.

Caught up in Contracts

Along the way Cindy found that there were bigger problems than tricky celebrities for an exhibiting artist. These spokes in the wheel really were make or break moments that made Cindy doubt if the big auction night would even go ahead. With celebrities confirmed and paintings approved, the next step was to find an ideal launch venue with enough space for an auction. She found a partner in a relatively new hotel in New York, the Hudson, which opened in 2000 and belonged to American entrepreneur Ian Schrager. Known for his ground-breaking concepts in real estate, he is credited for co-creating the 'boutique hotel' category of accommodation.

Cindy was naturally delighted to secure such a partner; she would stay at the hotel for a two-day PR blitz before displaying the celebrity paintings on the hip roof-top terrace at the hotel. But this was to be her first interaction with the American contract, tightly written to avoid litigation down the line.

Somewhere in-between changing Jack's nappies, cooking chicken nuggets and working on the half-finished paintings, Cindy received the contract. One particular requirement was to protect against Cindy from potentially saying or doing anything libellous (with lawsuits so common in the States) which confused her; she wasn't sure why it was there, and she didn't have the slightest idea what to do.

It immediately set the panic alight in Cindy's brain, already frazzled by dyslexia and motherhood, and for a moment she was prepared to throw in the towel, when a knock on the door came. Cindy had forgotten she had invited her friend Michele Lomnitz and her daughter to lunch, who just so happened to be American. Forced to confess her woes

(Cindy admits she was a very poor host that afternoon) Cindy showed her the contract and explained that she just didn't know what to do next. It was too late in the process to find another hotel, but she simply couldn't understand what it was asking and knew never to put her name to a contract without fully understanding it first.

The more the pair looked it over, the more Cindy's concern changed from worry to sheer panic. Time was running out and hadn't she got enough to do? School runs, celebrities to deal with and now an upcoming – and potentially expensive – show in New York that she would probably need a lawyer for before she even stepped foot in the country. Time wasn't on her side; how long would getting the right legal advice actually take her?

But as luck would have it, Michele had someone in mind that could help. She gave her the number of a solicitor for a U.S. firm with an office in London. Upon hearing Cindy's plight, one of the top lawyers immediately scrutinised the contract and gave her the go ahead to sign it. Knowing what Cindy was trying to achieve, he didn't charge her a penny, which she was incredibly grateful for. To Cindy, it is important to have people in your corner that you can trust. And just like, the show would go on.

Sir Richard Branson and Virgin Atlantic

Now that the hotel was taken care of, there was still the issue of getting a number of large canvases over the pond. It wasn't until a nail-biting eight weeks before her departure that Cindy learned she had received sponsorship for her journey. British entrepreneur, Sir Richard Branson, was the owner of

Virgin Atlantic and what's more, Cindy had already painted his dog Coco previously, an eight-year-old female that was a mix of Labrador and Irish Water Spaniel.

As the months ticked by and the paintings began to finish one by one, Cindy was having sleepless nights thinking that she would have to pay to ship them all over to America. While going by sea would be cheaper, there simply wasn't time as the months ticked down to the auction event on May 19th, 2003. Without a sponsor, the shipping costs alone were something unthinkable that could sink the show before it had even begun. But Sir Richard Branson not only threw Cindy a lifeline to take care of the shipping in full, but he came back shortly afterwards and offered Cindy a new opportunity. Virgin Atlantic were looking to launch a new pet friendly scheme and he thought that Cindy offered a unique service. Cindy says,

> "Virgin Atlantic were so great to me; not only did they ship all of my paintings – which were incredibly heavy – but Sir Richard Branson also told me how much he liked my work, and we later got together to work on a new project with the airline directly, *Flying Paws*. I will be forever thankful to the team for helping me get everything across so that the DOGNY project, which meant so much to me, was able to happen."

Virgin Atlantic – Flying Paws

Modest and philanthropic by nature, Cindy loves working with charities and is always thrilled and surprised when her paintings sell at charity auctions. That she can donate large sums of money to organisations in need and close to her heart, through art, is something she will never tire of. Yet, she has also been involved in work for corporate companies like Virgin, when she was personally asked by Sir Richard Branson to be part of his *Flying Paws* initiative which launched on the 1st of May 2005.

The reward scheme meant that jet-setting cats, dogs and even ferrets could collect 'paw prints' in the form of a stamp each time they travelled, allowing their owners to redeem special gifts. For those animals crossing time zones regularly, once they had racked up twenty paw prints, they had the option to commission a personal pawtrait from Cindy for free. The in-flight pet menu read:

Fancy your pawtrait on the wall for all to admire? 20 paw print stamps will earn you the unique opportunity to commission world renowned artist Cindy Lass to paint your pawtrait. Too shy or no room left on your wall? Then you can donate £200 or the local currency equivalent to your favourite animal charity or sanctuary or reward your human friend with 1000 bonus flying club miles.

Of the scheme's launch Branson said: "*This reward scheme is unlike any other and will set a precedent amongst the four-legged frequent flyers – after all, it is the pawtastic club to belong to!*"

Cindy, who produced several pawtraits thanks to the deal, stayed in touch with the end goal which, for her, was critical. She said:

"Virgin is a fabulous company and I love the thought of being involved with something like this right from the very beginning. If someone enjoys my work when they look upon it and it creates a good feel factor then I know I have achieved something."

Appearing on the *Today* show, NBC

Once the plane had touched down and Cindy had made it to the Hudson alongside Jill, who had flown out early with Cindy to help her set up and be on hand, Cindy could be excused for thinking that the rest of the event would be quite straightforward. Alas, this was not to be. Before Cindy had left London for the show, she had been invited onto the *Today* show, a TV programme for the NBC channel with star host Katie Couric. Worried that perhaps the preparation would be a lot for her, Roger – who would join Cindy and Jill with older son Ollie in a few days – asked sweetly if she would be OK on live TV to around 3.2 million Americans who would be tuning in for breakfast, a thought which could have sobered the most confident performer. Without hesitation, Cindy replied that yes, of course she would be fine. One thing Corona had taught her was confidence after all.

Arriving at the Hudson after a long flight, Cindy knew that to be on her best she needed a good night's sleep. The room she was sharing with Jill was sleek and modern, but its white walls with no cupboards did confuse the two slightly. Jill was wondering where to put the coats when Cindy noticed two hooks on the door and pointed to them. As Jill went to hang them up her hand bent strangely and she cried out. Cindy's first reaction was to laugh as it looked so strange, but she could see it wasn't something Jill had done by herself and described it as someone grabbing her fingers and yanking her hand up. Although it was a bizarre incident it made total sense to Cindy as energetically, there was spirit there with them. But Jill suffered with a bent little finger for the rest of her life.

This was just one of the strange events to happen on their trip to New York. The next morning, Cindy woke up to a phone call from the *Today* show. "*Hi, Cindy, just to let you know that although we wanted you on the show, we actually don't need you anymore.*"

Woken early and crushed with disappointment, Cindy found it hard to keep the frustration inside. Hadn't she just flown halfway around the world for this? "*No! I'm not having that,*" she retorted. She knew that the success of the charity auction was riding on a big audience such as the *Today* show tuning in. She insisted on speaking to the producer and, somehow managed to twist their arm and keep her slot. Next thing she knew he was promising a car to bring her to the studio and so once ready, she headed downstairs with Jill to her audience with America.

But once inside the car, Jill shouted that her ring was missing, left back in their room on the 16th floor. A priceless antique diamond and white gold Russian ring she had been given by Harold. They had not gone more than a few feet before Cindy insisted on stopping and running back to the hotel, despite the possibility of being late for the programme. Once in the lobby and amongst the huge bank of elevators, the first one she ran for miraculously held a maintenance worker from the hotel, who soon called a plumber. After ten minutes of frantic searching, they found it in the u-bend of the basin. Another ten minutes and the plumber estimated that it would have been washed away and impossible to retrieve. Cindy was quick to tell him how incredibly grateful she was, although she truly believes it was fate that put them together that day – completely out of her hands. With no cash on her at the time, she was quick to return to the reception later to leave him a $100 bill, something guided her to the knowledge that this was the least she could do.

Finally, after the mad dash of the morning Cindy and Jill arrived at the studio where Jill soon settled into life in the green room – Cindy could hardly get her out afterwards! But Cindy's ordeal wasn't over yet. After all that had already gone wrong, she was told that actually, her segment wouldn't be live with Katie Couric as planned, but with news anchor Ann Curry instead. She was crushed as Katie was someone who she thought would be very sensitive to the cause. Instead, when she met Ann just before the pair went live, Ann was quick to get under Cindy's skin saying, "*I don't really like dogs or artists.*" With "*Three, two, one!*" in her ear, Cindy felt her nerves disappear and a fire burn brightly in her belly – thinking to herself "*If this lady doesn't like dogs or artists, she is going to be given an education in the next two-and-a-half-minutes!*" And so, she did. Looking Ann straight in the eyes and hardly letting her get a word in edge ways, Cindy was not only engaging, but also bubbly, making sure to promote the charity and the auction dates. A dream guest.

Once her part was done, the producer thanked her for standing her ground. In fact, the programme made a great TV segment. For the first time Cindy allowed herself to relax

– things were on a roll, this charity auction was going to be another great success, she could feel it.

But reality soon came crashing down. After all the hassle of getting the paintings ready, then losing her mum's ring and facing down a negative presenter live on television, she was completely exhausted. But there was no time to relax. Her pawtraits were going to be displayed on the Sky terrace of the Hudson Hotel that evening and she still needed to set everything up. A huge job to man-handle, unwrap and set up her twenty-plus large pawtraits in place.

That was when Cindy remembered that help was at hand, a friend's brother – Jason – lived in New York and was able to help set up at the last minute. But it was only thousands of miles away from her comfort zone that Cindy realised the enormity of the task ahead.

George Whipple

Later that evening, her whirlwind tour of the US press didn't stop, and she moved from *Good Morning America* to being interviewed at the Hudson by TV station NY1. Presenter George Whipple brought his own dog, Jackie Ruckles, to the show while recording a live interview with Cindy. It was watched by her mother Jill, babysitting Ollie who had just arrived (Jack was back in London, too young for such a long flight), who credited it as one of her proudest moments, sitting in the hotel room and watching her daughter on the TV.

In his interview, George asked: "*Tell me about some of these stars that you've painted, what dogs have you painted here tonight?*"

Standing in front of Cate Blanchett's white terrier puppy painting of Egg, Cindy replied:

"Oh every type of dog! To Ivana Trump's Yorkshire terrier and toy poodle and Heidi Klum's Jack Russell. I think I've done about seventy-five dogs in all.

"I'm from England and I wanted to bring some sunshine over to you because I think you're all wonderful people. I wanted to make the world a safer place by having funds aside to help these wonderful volunteer people to help look after the dogs who do such amazing jobs and keep us all safe and happy."

Whipple made the joke that she must now be 'dog tired' but Cindy explained that the paintings were being auctioned off to help DOGNY, for dogs who were wounded and depressed after their experience of working throughout 9/11. The money would pay for specialist showers to help clean animals in future, while also going towards veterinary care where needed.

George also asked about her first work for DOGNY, the fibreglass German Shepherd. He was quick to pick up on the vibrant colours of the dog's eyes, the blue colours and the daisies. Cindy tried to explain that it was just something she felt she had to paint, and when that urge came – she knew that everything would turn out okay as long as she followed her feelings, or spirit as she calls it.

CHAPTER 6

PAINTING FOR HRH: HER MAJESTY THE QUEEN

Receiving the Phone Call

In early 2006 and now known as a first-class animal artist having finished her work painting pawtraits for Battersea and DOGNY, Cindy received an unexpected commission request by telephone. It was a call that would turn out to be completely life-changing for Cindy, taking her work and presence in the art world to a new level.

The client was Her Majesty Queen Elizabeth and the lady on the telephone was one of the queen's ladies-in-waiting. It was the year before Elizabeth's 80th birthday and the monarch, having been recommended Cindy's distinct style of animal portraiture, was keen to have her beloved dogs captured on canvas by the artist to commemorate her special day. Cindy was stunned by the request but naturally agreed without hesitation, feeling incredibly honoured at such a unique commission.

The queen is well-known for her love of the Welsh Corgi, a breed that she was surrounded by growing up before being gifted her very own corgi, Susan, who was a present from her father, King George VI, on her eighteenth birthday in 1944. Susan was said to go everywhere with Elizabeth, and even accompanied her on her honeymoon in Hampshire.

On that initial phone call between Cindy and the lady-in-waiting, the pair discussed how a sitting might be managed, but with two packed diaries to work against them, Cindy agreed to once again paint from photographs. The lady-in-waiting asked Cindy lots of questions about how long her paintings usually take to complete so that should try and pencil in a date when the queen might be available to receive the painting, but Cindy wasn't able to give a rough estimation – this was a piece of work she would have to fit into other projects alongside her busy life now that the boys were growing up; she simply couldn't give a date from a single phone call. The lady-in-waiting was slightly unhappy about this, but the pair agreed to catch up once Cindy had managed to start and agree a plan from there.

A week or so later when the photographs arrived, Cindy saw that there was actually quite a number of dogs, seven to be precise. Four of the dogs were distinctively corgis – Linnet, Monty, Holly and Willow – but when she studied the photos, there were three other dogs of a breed that she simply couldn't place. Never one to be shy, Cindy picked up the phone and got through to one of the ladies-in-waiting. Cindy explains,

> "I said to the lady on the phone that there was a dog in the bottom left-hand corner of one of the photos that

was confusing me as it didn't quite look like a corgi. In a very clipped and posh voice, the lady-in-waiting went on to tell me that what I was looking at was called a dorgi. I kept waiting for her to laugh but very seriously and slowly she said, *"that is what happens when a corgi has a relationship with a daschund, and we call that a dorgi."* I was shocked! All I could say was, oh right..."

She confirmed that Cider, Candy and Berry were all in fact, dorgis. Little did Cindy know at the time, but the young queen had helped introduce dorgis as a popular breed in Great Britain after mating her corgi, Tiny, with her sister Princess Margaret's dachshund called Pipkin.

The issue of the date was raised again but at that point in time, Cindy's approach to the painting process was fluid and emotive. She was tapping in more to where her desire to paint came from, a force from within that was not something she could necessarily perform to a strict schedule or tight deadline. Integral to each piece of artwork Cindy creates is her insightful ability to pick up on the energy of her four-legged subjects, which takes careful and painstaking study. Besides, painting is Cindy's window of calm, her solace and time-out from all the stresses of the world; to constrain that creative process with dates or deadlines would make it much harder for the energy to flow. Therefore, and with such an important commission, she found it impossible to put an exact time length on its completion. Although her mother begged Cindy to put a date in the queen's diary, she was adamant. She reasons:

"I can't paint when I don't feel like painting; it's like waiting until you feel yourself getting hungry to enjoy a good meal. Once those tastebuds start salivating each bite will be wonderful, and that's how I feel about painting – I have to be patient until I feel a hunger for it and then I know the magic will happen."

She preferred to wait until she was finished and happy with the painting before agreeing a delivery date, even if this meant Her Majesty wouldn't be available to receive it in person. Besides, what would she do once she handed it over? Cindy couldn't see herself curtseying and taking tea with the queen, she felt it would have been a waste of an opportunity. Luckily, Cindy had a better idea…

A Sad Time

At the time of the royal commission, Cindy was heavily involved with donating her time to another charity, this time the University College London Hospital, although this particular branch of her working life was born from heart-breaking circumstances.

In summer 1999, a few days before her first son Oliver turned two, Cindy was at home preparing to host a special party with the whole family for his birthday. It was rare for them all to get together and after years of renovating, the new house in St John's Wood with a conservatory and garden was finally ready and perfect for hosting. Cindy had also passed her twelve-week mark and was feeling happy and secure in her second pregnancy. Only, the day before the big occasion, she started bleeding at home.

After being the go-ahead by the hospital to go back home, Roger took Ollie out for lunch and Cindy stayed at home. She remembers the pains getting worse and being stuck on the floor of the bathroom. She simply couldn't get up. Roger arrived just as she tragically miscarried in their en-suite bathroom. As the pair took in the tragedy, they decided to call the ambulance as Cindy remained weak and was still bleeding. She had the foresight and courage to wrap the baby and bring it with them in a bag so that the medical team could understand why it had happened.

After admitting Cindy and stopping the bleeding, Cindy remembers being left in a waiting room while in a wheelchair, looking at grey and dreary walls for hours while waiting for a procedure that would ensure everything was out of her system. She felt lost, empty and too exhausted to grieve. In fact, she would have dearly loved for some sort of distraction to help her through the long wait. It was there that Cindy vowed to try and make this experience better for the next person. Whether it was a half-finished piece of embroidery that women could help to weave a few stitches while they waited, or interesting and thoughtful paintings on the wall to look at. With nothing to do but think about what could have been, Cindy simply longed for colour.

Feeling frustrated – how after going through such a shattering event they were kept waiting for so long, when all they wanted to do was go home and process it together, Roger and Cindy asked a passing porter what was causing the delay. He sat down and explained that a seventeen-year-old girl had come in on her own in a similar situation to Cindy. With no-one to help or hold her hand, the porter himself had stayed with her and the medical team had prioritised her situation. The young girl had subsequently had her procedure and gone home, alone.

Even in the midst of her own personal sadness and grief, Cindy was struck by how unfriendly an environment the hospital was for such tragedies, something which would be felt even more starkly at such a young age with no one there to support them. The generous porter explained how he had stayed with the girl for as long as he could, something Cindy couldn't be angry about; at least that girl had someone for a short while. But she doubled down on that mental note to do something to help.

Cindy discovered that the hospital was involved with Paintings in Hospitals, an initiative which raises funds for art and art groups in hospitals, aswell as loaning its own collection of art. Its headquarters were in the West End, and so she found some of her spare paintings in the garage (where she kept any canvases that wouldn't fit in her office) and immediately donated two of them to the charity as an interim measure.

The next day, Oliver turned two years old, and Cindy threw herself into birthday preparations, not really giving herself any time to grieve the loss of her second baby. She was open and frank with everyone about her experience. While many gave her their sympathy there was one acquaintance she bumped into locally who made a remark that felt almost spiteful to Cindy. "*Oh you don't look like someone who's just had a miscarriage – you look great!*" might have been said in good faith, but it hurt Cindy. Because she was a woman who had just lost a baby, and no matter how she talked or what she looked like, nothing would change that fact. And now she needed to go and put a brave face on for her son and the rest of her family. It felt exhausting.

Volunteering at UCH

Fortunately, Cindy went on to have a second son, Jack, who was born a full year later in September 2000. The following year, Cindy was holidaying in Spain with family and the newest addition, when a lady called Lunette tapped Cindy on the shoulder and told her that she loved her artwork and could she help a local charity. At the time Cindy was halfway through lunch with her kids. But she asked the lady to wait for her and afterwards Cindy went over to hear more.

The charity gala night was on behalf of the children's cancer unit at University College Hospital (UCH) part of University College London Hospitals (UCLH). If she would only donate a painting, it would go towards supporting funds raised at the department's annual charity evening at The Four Seasons hotel on Park Lane. At this point in her career, Cindy's paintings could command up to £10,000 each when auctioned off and so Cindy found herself in the very fortunate position where she was able to help and support such vital organisations. Once she had got the boys' lunch sorted, all she could say was yes!

A few months later on a rainy evening, it was time to attend the gala at The Four Seasons. Getting dressed up and going out was the last thing she wanted to do; she had just got back from New York after helping paint the German

Shephard fibreglass and once the kids were in bed, Cindy felt like joining them. But Jill insisted she had her hair done and suggested that perhaps a night out was exactly what Cindy needed – a bit of a tonic after such a hectic few months.

Reluctantly Cindy agreed, and her mood lifted once she felt a little more glamorous. But the evening would take a strange turn, Cindy would only get as far as checking her coat in when a gentleman called Guy Noble made a beeline for her and introduced himself. He was the arts curator for UCLH and amazingly had spotted the paintings she had purposely left at Paintings in Hospitals. It was his intent to hang both of them in the pregnancy ward – would Cindy like to come and see them? All of a sudden, a wave of grief hit her. She remembered feeling so determined to help the poor families that found themselves in such a predicament, and without doing anything but leaving a donation, suddenly her paintings would find themselves on the way to her chosen destination. It was too much for Cindy to take, she made her apologies and dashed off to the ladies' room where all she could do was cry for the baby that never was. Times like this are part of the reason why Cindy thinks our energies can play a huge part in our future. Cindy's grief was so raw when sat there in the hospital, her thoughts so purposeful – *I will help this hospital* – that even without trying too hard her wish had come true. Eventually she composed herself, and went out to speak more with Guy and apologise for running away so suddenly.

She explained that her chance meeting with the man who had not only chosen her paintings but was also planning to put them in the very place she had in mind, was the perfect storm. All of the grief and pain from Cindy's miscarriage that she had been holding onto and suppressing for a while, rose to the fore. The timing was bittersweet – it also happened to be the date the baby would have turned two-years-old. When Guy heard her story, he was touched and asked her to meet him at the hospital the next day to discuss a project he had in mind.

They met in the entrance hall, a rather drab and 'down in the mouth' looking place that was in desperate need of a colour injection. Guy described how the trust had ideally wanted a bright and cheerful mural at the entrance however, because the building was government-owned, there was a fair amount of red tape which ultimately meant that it had to be returned in the same condition once the lease was up. Together they took a little tour of some of the wards and discussed at length various options that might work, including a possible mural on the radiology ward, so there was something cheerful to look at whilst waiting for treatment.

Unfortunately, due to similar restrictions the mural was also not to be, but the pair came to a different agreement. Between Cindy's incredibly busy work schedule and caring for her own children, she didn't have a lot of spare time. But determined to help in some way, she agreed to come in once a week on a Thursday, to sit and paint with some of the very sick children, most who were terminally ill, as part of the hospital school.

Here Cindy would draw, paint and stimulate the little ones into having fun with art. In many ways it allowed them to open up and discuss their own hopes and fears. There were lots of great conversations, and equally days when all Cindy wanted to do was cry after a visit. She felt so much love for the children.

◄ **Cindy's Early Family (1968) – Jill, Jack, Craig, Cindy and Tracy Grant**

Happy times in Cindy's first house in White Lodge Close, The Bishops Avenue. Cindy: "I am so proud of my Dad, he was a self made business man who built and designed his own beautiful house."

solute Beginners (1985) – Cindy Lass, tree Studios car park ▶

ıdy's outfit from Absolute Beginners. Cindy: 'e never met a star as charasmatic and ırming as David Bowie."

▼ **Corona Stage School (1976) – Karen Corti, Cindy Grant, Jayne Tottman, Jo Skinner, Joanna Harris**

Ravenscourt Park in the playground at Corona Academy, the tree was the central feature.

Love of Cindy's Life and Soul Partner 95) – Roger and Cindy Lass

wly-weds Cindy and Roger, taken just 'ore their summer party. Behind them tures Cindy's painting of a window on their ing room wall.

◀ **Cindy's Fam[ily] Hubby and S[ons] (2018) – Roger, Cin[dy] Ollie and Jack Lass**

Out in the East E[nd] of London for sun[day] lunch, rare family ti[me] together that Cin[dy] loves.

▼ **Ascot (1992) – Roger and Cindy Lass**
Ascot races in the Queen's enclosure, Cindy has been a regular from 12 years old.

A bride's Right wedding in a polling station

BRIDE Cindy Grant, 21, was all agog when she arrived at a synagogue to take her vows yesterday – it was being used as a polling station.

Cindy, wearing a stunning white bridal gown, dashed past bemused onlookers to cast her vote before tying the knot just yards away with bridegroom Ashley Lass.

The booth was set up in the entrance of the synagogue in London's Hampstead Garden Suburb.

Cindy said: "I feel very lucky to be able to kill two birds with one stone." Asked who she voted for, she replied: "Shall I just say, 'something old, something new, something borrowed, something blue.'"

▲ **Wedding Day (1992) – Cindy Lass**
Cindy drops in to vote before her wedding, makes page 3 of *The Sun* but mistakenly h[as] her married to her father-in-law, Ashley. [It] still makes her giggle.

▲ **Anita and Jill (1998) – Anita Dobson and Jill Grant**
Once Cindy had introduced them the pair were always firm friends who enjoyed each others company for many years.

▲ **Happy Vibrations (1995) – Tamar and Dave Murray, brother Craig Grant and Roger Lass**
Tamar and Dave joined Cindy's family for a fabulous chinese barbecue when they were living at Ordanance Hill - those were the pre-children days!

Yellow Gerbera (2004) – Cindy Lass ▶

The late Philip Somerville helped Cindy to design this hat but what Cindy's remembers most is the green flies it attracted all day long. *Credit: Ken Towner and Aubrey Hart*

▼ **First Mixed Show (2005) – Cindy Lass and Barbara Grundy**

For Cindy having Barbara Grundy believe in her and support her first debut will always be a proud moment.

▼ **The Contemporary Art Group (1994) Cindy Lass, Jill Grant and Harold Laurier**

An amazing moment for Cindy and family Ebury Street. Cindy: "It was surreal to see that ▮ paintings were actually hanging and then so▮ the beginning of my art career."

◀ **The Model (2000) – Cindy Lass**

Here an award-winning photograph of Cind▮ hands by Andreas Heumann graces the fro▮ cover of Photographer magazine. *Credit: Andre▮ Heumann*

First Solo Show (1995) – Andrew
ningsby, Ellie and Bernie from
nic PR

dy: "A fantastic opening of my
ut solo show thanks to a great team."

e Wonderful Barbara Windsor
95) – Barbara Windsor and
ndy Lass ▶

dy and Barbara Windsor at the
ening of Cindy's exhibition at The
ningsby Gallery. Cindy, "With
bs and her lovely hubby Scott
re it made the energy glamous and
iting." *Credit: Ortho*

◀ Second Solo Show – Anita
Dobson and Cindy Lass
(1997)
Friends Cindy and Anita
come together to enjoy
another of Cindy's solo
shows, Anita was the first
person after her family that
Cindy told she was four-
months pregnant with Ollie.
Credit: PA Images

▲ **Energetic House (2000) – Uri Geller, Cindy Lass and dogs**
Together with Uri Geller, Jon Jon and Chico. Cindy, "There were brilliant crystals in his house a car outside that was covered in bent forks, such an amazing force there."

▼ **Uri Geller (2001) – Cindy Lass and Uri Geller**
Cindy is able to show Uri his painting in the flesh at Home House in support of Battersea Dogs Home. They had a great connection and Uri told Cindy that he loved her work.

▲ **Legend (2003) – Chita Rivera Cindy Lass**
Cindy saw Chita back stage on broad after her tango with Antonio Bandera Nine. Cindy: "It was the sexiest Tango and my Mum had ever seen."

▲ **New York and Celebrity Pawtraits Here She Comes! (2003) – George Whipple and Cindy Lass**

With George Whipple filming for a New York news channel on the roof of the Hudson Hotel.

▼ **Never to be Forgotten (2003) – Mary Bloom and Cindy Lass**

To Cindy, Mary was a both a beautiful soul and an amazing photographer, they became friends although Mary sadly passed in 2021.

▲ **A Special Time (2005) – Cindy Lass and Jill Grant**

Jill and Cindy spent a special few days together in the run up to the Celebrity Pawtrait exhibition in New York, in aid of charity DOGNY. Jill made it clear that she was so proud of Cindy, and loved joining her in her travels. *Credit: Getty Images*

▲ **Anita and the Boys (2003) – Anita Dobson, Jack Lass and Ollie Lass**
Aunty Neets with a young Jack and Ollie. They adored seeing her every year at the Pantomine!

▲ **The David Hockney (2002) David Hockey and Cindy Lass**
At the V & A exhibition Cin had a lovely chat with pain David Hockney. Cindy: "What fabulous, down-to-earth, humb and talented man. Beyond his tim

◀ **Away in Heaven (2011) – Cin in front of Mount Abu**
This was a life changing trip Cindy and Roger, they felt so mu love from Brahma Kumaris a Cindy has since welcomed its eth into her heart.

◄ Blue and White Vase (1994)

Cindy's first ever painting – the blue and white vase she framed for Jill who had it hung in pride of place right up until her death in late 2021. As she requested, it has now returned to Cindy .

∪nset Tulips (1994) ►

indy's favourite Sunset Tulips, and the rst painting that she went on to sell while Paddington Private tennis club.

◄ Cookie (1995)

The wonderful Cookie, gouche and water colour on paper. Cindy: "My adorable Cookie, this painting really helped me through her passing".

◀ **The Bench (1994)**
Painted while her father was in hospital, Cindy: "I knew I would never paint like this again. It was very emotional to paint through such stress."

Secret Garden (1994) ▶
Also painted while her father was in hospital, Cindy never realised that this technique was called Pointillism until much later.

◄ Blue, Blue and More Blue (1997)

First Jill and now Cindy have an affinity to the colour blue. Cindy: "I loved painting this huge canvas in my garden. Blue is such a colour of strength for me."

ᴜnflowers (1995) ►

ɪndy: "This looked great hanging in The ᴏom (the restaurant in the Halcyon hotel) though my Roger didn't want me to sell it. He sisted we keep it even though it could have ᴇen sold many times over."

◄ Lazy Lunch (1994)

Probably the still life that is most commented on, Cindy never realised that the writing was back to front due to her dyslexia.

▲ **The Queen's Corgis (2006)**
One of Cindy's greatest achievements. Cindy: "It made Mum so proud, I'm just delighted H
Majesty likes it and has it hanging in her private quarters." *Credit: Getty Images*

Happy Families (2019) – Ollie, Roger, Cindy and Jack Lass ▶

On holiday in Koh Sumui, Thailand, with her two (now adult sons) Ollie and Jack, Cindy was at her happiest. And if you look in the background, Roger makes a surprise appearance in the sea between Ollie's legs.

◀ **How Much is that Pawtrait in the Window? (2000) – Cindy Lass and Ollie Lass (three years old)**

At the launch of Oh Doggy perfume at Debenhams in Oxford Street. Cindy's paintings were borrowed to use in the display window and throughout the event. Cindy: "Ollie loved it!"

At Home with Jack (2004) – Cindy Lass and Jack Lass (three years old) ▶

Cindy would often give interviews or have photographers come round to shoot her latest work, but on this occasion she wasn't sure which she was most proud of, her latest painting or the giggling young child she had created.

◄ Tea for One (1996)
There is nothing more calming for Cin◖
than enjoying a pot of tea with so◖
gorgeous flowers to look at.

Kew Garden (1994) ►
After a visit to Kew Gardens, Cindy painted
this based on a photograph she took at the
time. One of her early paintings, this sold at
the Coningsby gallery and Cindy's only regret
is that she doesn't know where it has gone since.

**◄ Celebrity Pawtraits in Aid of Batters◖
Dogs Home (2000)**
Her first ever celebrity pawtrait, Cindy w◖
so relieved when David Furnish rang to t◖
her that both he and Sir Elton were bo◖
over the moon with the pawtrait – the sho◖
went on to be a phenomenal success and◖
great benefit to the charity.

◄ The Best Bulldog (2002)

Part of the original Celebrity Pawtraits, this painting then went on to be used for the Action on Addiction/ASK Pizza collaboration. Cindy: "Charlie Sheen kindly allowed me to paint a pawtrait of his dog Hank for the show, which he loved." Cindy never realised how popular Bulldog's were until after completing this pawtrait.

▲ Ralph (1998)

After Cookie, Roger wanted his own dog and having grown up with miniature Schnauzers it seemed obvious to get one. But the whole family adored him.

◄ The Parrots (1995)

A much sought-after Cindy Lass original, this painting has been sold on many times. Cindy doesn't know who the owner is to this day. A mystery.

▲ **Bien venue en mange (1997)**
This painting was commissioned by a friend
of Roger's who had a very big kitchen with
space to fill. He loved it.

Daily Mail and the Blue Hat (1997) ▶
With the aspects of this painting at odds
with each other, Cindy simply loves the
madness of it and relishes the freedom that
as the artist, the scene is hers to set.

◀ **Summer Breeze (1999)**
Now hanging in a villa in the South of Fra
and made all the sweeter by a friend spottin
and ringing to tell her. There are now Cindy I
originals all around the world.

◄ Table with Summer Flowers (1995)
Cindy: "I really enjoyed painting this commision for a house in Little Venice."

Doggy Evening in ~~M~~ayfair **(2018) – Jill Grant,** ~~Ro~~sanne Bennett and her ~~do~~g, **Cindy Lass with Flash,** ~~Ri~~chard Caring and Tracy ~~E~~min **►**

~~Ci~~ndy and friends enjoy their ~~an~~nual evening for private ~~me~~mbers and guests at the ~~Ge~~orge Club's doggy evening ~~in~~ Mayfair, Cindy would take ~~Fla~~sh everywhere with her ~~an~~d so these events allowed ~~pe~~t owners to put their four-~~leg~~ged friends first.

◄ Momo (1998) – Cindy Lass and Mourad Mazouz
Cindy with the owner of restaurant Momo and her painting that served as the invite for the Red Cross Ball. Cindy: "It was a fantastic evening, and together we raised loads of money for Red Cross."

▲ **Action on Addiction (2003) – Cindy Lass with finalists from the Ask Pizza challenge**
To support Action on Addiction by working with Ask Pizza, Cindy came up with this brilliant art competition while eating pizza, and this photo shows her with the winners. Cindy: "It was very difficult to judge but one of the most enjoyable things I've ever done."

▲ **Celebrity Flowers (2006) – Cindy Lass**
At the launch of Celebrity Flowers, a colourful show held in the Square One gallery. Cindy's unique hat is made from real flowers recently displayed at the Chelsea Garden Show and made by Moses Stevens. Each celebrity flowers painting was personally signed by its celebrity. *Credit: PA Images*

▲ **Great Evening (2005) – Richard O'Brien, Patricia Quinn and Cindy Lass**
Both Richard and Patricia signed their favourite flower painting that Cindy had designed in aid of Sir Elton John's Aids Foundation before a racuous evening in Cindy's house. She thinks they're both fantastic and that Richard has a wicked sense of humour.

◀ **Filming (2005) – Emma Thompson**
Cindy eventually managed to track down Emma on set at her trailer so that she could sign the painting of her favourite flower, encrusted with Swarovski crystals.

All Our Hearts Beat As One (2012) – Cindy Lass, Adam Wilkie and Graham Rebak ▶
Cindy with her amazing friend Adam and his husband Graham. Cindy: "Friends are everything in life and both of them have been hugely supportive for my first *All Our Hearts Beat As One* show."

All Our Hearts Beat As One Celebrity Edition (2016) – Cindy Lass, Jo Wood and Debbie Moore ▶

All Our Heats Beat As One – the celebrity edition. Cindy: "That night there was fantastic energy and fabulous art work to enjoy from 55 celebrites and 60 different artists within the gallery. Simply amazing."

◀ Soul Sisters (2016) – Nikk Newman and Cindy Lass

Cindy and Nikki get ready for the gallery exhibition at Cindy's home together. Cindy: "I can't thank my friends enough for all their help along the way." *Credit: Laraine Krantz*

Hearts and More Hearts (2016) – Jon Moss and Cindy Lass ▶

Cindy with Jon Moss, drummer in Culture Club. Cindy: "Gallery DIFFERENT was an amazing space to host this show and it was so lovely to be supported by so many good friends."

Anne Had No Time to Blossom; Everyone Has the Right to Blossom (2008)

Inspired by the tree that Anne Frank would look upon whilst in hiding, Cindy decided to paint it in full blossom. Cindy: "This was the most emotional painting I have ever painted, yet I am so humbled and proud that I was asked." I knew it was important painting with the message it carried for the next generation."

▲ **Anne Frank's Sapling (2008) – Cindy Lass and Emma Thompson**
Cindy visited Emma at home to show her the painting and receive a glance at the sapling that had been presented to Emma. Cindy: "This journey has allowed me to meet some amazing people. With Emma, I just love how natural she is and her kind thoughts about the world." *Credit: Mike Fear*

▼ **Museum of Tolerance (2018** **Cindy Lass and Morris Price**
After the hanging of Cindy's Every Has the Right to Blossom paint Cindy met an unbelievable holoc surivior – Morris Price, and wa touched by his story. *Credit: Reb Duke*

◀ **Holland Park (2008) – Cindy Lass and Michael Win**
On what would have been Anne Frank's 79th birth Cindy gathered friends to plant a tree in Holland P and local celebrity Michael Winner kindly unve Cindy's painting, Everyone Has the Right to Bloss *Credit: Alamy*

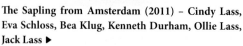

The Sapling from Amsterdam (2011) – Cindy Lass, Eva Schloss, Bea Klug, Kenneth Durham, Ollie Lass, Jack Lass ▶
At Universty College School planting one of the last saplings cultivated from the tree outside Anne Frank's hiding place. Cindy: "A very wonderful and emotional day planting the sapling in U.C.S. grounds where my boys went to school." *Credit: Viv Yeo*

◄ Hasn't He Grown Up… (2005) – Paul Bettany and Cindy Lass

Cindy bumped into Paul at the Film Critics awards, she hadn't seen him since he was eight years old. Cindy: "He's turned into a kind and handsome man." *Credit: Mark Moody*

ıcy Dress (2014) – Cindy Lass and Michelle Collins ►

er working together for charity, the pair became good
nds. This photo was taken when the duo were on
r way to a Halloween party with families and wanted
lress in the spirit.

◄ Primrose Hill Girls (2018) – Neeley Moore, Cindy Lass and Meg Matthews

Neighbours and friends, Meg is a huge fan of Cindy's work and has supported Cindy on numerous occassions, from gallery openings to walks with the dog.

st Friends Re-Unite (2016) – Tamar Murray
1 Cindy Lass ►

er dinner at Watts Gallery, Cindy and Tamar
ch up over a few glasses. Cindy: "Special times
h my special friend Tamar."

▲ **Good Friends (1997) – Larry Adler and Cindy Lass**
One of Larry and Cindy's many nights out together, this one took place at the Grosvenor Hotel in the Gallery bar for Cindy's solo art show.

▲ **The Best Present (2004) – Cindy Lass**
A signed print from celebrity photographer Jo Stoddart who had the great idea to photogra Cindy's paintings in a more sensual mann What he didn't know was that Cindy was turni 40, and seeing herself differently – confident a sexy – was the best birthday present she co give to herself.

▲ **Irreplaceable (2008) – Jill Grant and Cindy Lass**
Jill has always been Cindy's biggest supporter but sadly died while this book was being written. Cindy: "There was, and will never be, nobody quite like Jilly Grant."

▲ **Forever Connected (2012) – Jenny Seagro and Cindy Lass**
Cindy and Jenny are good friends who ha both supported each others charity work. Jen agrees: "We are all from the same source."

But overall, it was a rewarding moment in Cindy's week, and she remembers one little girl in particular who was having a very difficult time and wasn't eating. Her mother worked full-time, and her father was a lorry driver, so rarely at home. The family were really struggling financially, to the point where they were using their credit card purely to buy food to eat. Because of the need to keep working and the distance they lived from the hospital, this absolutely gorgeous little girl was often on her own in the hospital, not eating and refusing to talk to anyone. The situation broke Cindy's heart and, in her empathetic and caring way, she was drawn to the girl. She made sure to spend time with her when in on a Thursday, making it clear there was absolutely no pressure for her to talk but just to have company and, slowly, the trust built up between them. A breakthrough came. Cindy exclaims:

> "I don't know what I said, but she started to pick up the pencil that I had and began to draw."

At that time, UCH was struggling to gain publicity for fundraisers as sister hospital Great Ormond Street had a much higher profile, including more celebrity endorsements and was therefore able to provide better equipment and a more supportive environment for its young patients. Until then, Cindy had deliberately not involved herself with any hospital politics; however, by this point, she had met another little girl who she felt needed her support. The little girl's father had died from a brain tumour and her illness was more of a mental issue than physical, which the medical team felt would be better addressed at Great Ormond Street, only no transfer was available. Cindy felt so strongly that this little girl would benefit from a move to Great Ormond Street, it became her mission to not only get her relocated – with all the red tape that would involve – but to also raise funds for the UCH ward to improve the facility with additional crafts, games and electronics for all of the children staying there.

In true Lass fashion, Cindy set the wheels in motion by discussing the situation with an influential friend, Annabel Schild, who agreed and was prepared to raise a lot of money for the hospital. Unfortunately, and quite inexplicably, the hospital's board members vetoed the idea. Undeterred, a few weeks later Cindy and her friend returned to the hospital with funds they had raised, only to be told that the money couldn't be earmarked for a specific project, it would have to go to the group as a whole and then doled out where required the most. Potentially leapfrogging the children's wing. Frustrated, Cindy informed the Trust in no uncertain terms, that the little girl she had been working so closely with on her weekly visits needed to be moved to Great Ormond Street, threatening to take the story to the press if action wasn't taken. Thankfully, the girl was transferred that very day, however, Cindy felt she couldn't carry on working with UCH after that. She left because she couldn't bear the politics.

As this all was playing out, Cindy received the call from the lady-in-waiting. Before she left her schoolroom at UCH for good Cindy had the great idea to take the children with her to Buckingham Palace and deliver her painting to the queen together. But first of all, Cindy had to finish it ready for the queen's birthday in June. Eventually, she found the inner calm she needed to complete the massive 5ft x 4ft acrylic painting on canvas and rang the lady-in-waiting to set a date.

Arriving at Buckingham Palace

Having commissioned a special medical bus to take the children, Cindy accompanied them from the hospital to Buckingham Palace to present the enormous canvas on the 13th July 2006. Her work had taken six months and while Cindy was happy with her creation, there was still a little trepidation for such an important commission. Having never trained as an artist, it always amazed her somewhat that something that had started out as a hobby had quickly become so much more than that. Never once had she imagined she would be presenting Her Majesty Queen Elizabeth II with one of her paintings. Cindy explains her thought process along the way.

"I was never able to really consider who I was painting for because I was really up against it with everything else and had done my fair share of celebrity paintings by that point. Once I started with the outline it sort of just stuck – although I actually didn't know much about corgi's before I started, I thought they looked more like gremlins in the early stages – but they looked great by the time I finished. What I paint is what I paint. I can only paint what I feel and see. There's something in my brain that means what I've painted goes out looking exactly like it should. I've only ever painted over one painting, the rest I have left well alone."

On arrival at the palace on a lovely sunny morning in July, Cindy and the children were directed to the queen's private entrance. Cindy had decided against wearing a dress, something she's not always comfortable with, and went with smart trousers and a tailored jacket – and a good choice it was as it meant Cindy could attend to the children's needs where necessary without worrying about not looking presentable. The bus was met by a lady-in-waiting, a butler in a red tailcoat who looked very sharp, and a photographer who was there to greet them as Cindy displayed the astonishing, five-foot canvas created to honour the queen on her eightieth birthday, celebrating some of her most beloved dogs.

Having been unable to give the palace a completion date, the queen was not available to receive the painting in person and although, in hindsight, Cindy would have loved to have met Elizabeth, she did not regret her reasons for being unable to comply on this point. She expresses, a little ruefully:

> "It's not the way the spirit works with me when I'm painting – I just have to follow its rules! Once I got to the end it was perfect. Even so, as I signed the bottom, I felt nerves in my stomach. I don't think of myself as an artist; I am just a woman living in this world. If my energy makes someone else smile, what else can I live for?"

> "But most importantly that day was about not letting the kids down. Getting the bus together and making sure it was kitted out with medical equipment and snacks for the children was a tremendous challenge, but seeing their faces more than made up for it. I know that my mum Jill was also really, really

proud of me. Even though she's now gone, I think at the time she quickly realised the enormity of such a day and how it would be a defining moment of my career. When it was over it hit me and she said that I was 'strutting like a peacock' – she really was over the moon and delighted for me."

While it was a fabulous morning for the children from her schoolroom, there was one child who couldn't make it due to ill health at the last minute. When Cindy spoke to her later that day she was so upset to have missed it and so, perhaps a little naively, Cindy promised that she would take her personally back to the palace to see the painting. The next day, Cindy rang the lady-in-waiting to explain and ask if she could pop in with the little girl very quickly. Shocked, the lady-in-waiting replied that it was hanging in the queen's own private quarters, but she was happy to report back that it had made the queen smile when she saw it. Grateful that Elizabeth was pleased with her work, Cindy replied a little nonchalantly,

"Oh that's OK. We'll just run in and run out. Can you take it off the wall and bring it down to us so that we can see it. Maybe you can let them know we're coming?"

Once she had recovered, the lady-in-waiting explained that no-one was allowed to simply breeze into the queen's private quarters, least of all take things from the wall to swap for later. The security and protocol needed would be much lengthier than simply 'popping in'. If one can even 'pop in' to Buckingham Palace. Understandably, Cindy then had to break her promise to the young girl, and the look on her face meant that to this day, Cindy has never promised something that she isn't positive she can deliver. Still, Cindy felt over the moon that her work had made the queen smile and that she was so taken with it she had had it hung in her own private quarters so that she could look at it every day.

Recently, Cindy was contacted by a journalist from the BBC, who was lucky enough to be invited to Buckingham Palace. With restrictions due to the pandemic, he had to wear a mask, Jill suggested to make people happy during such sad times Cindy should make a print of the queen's corgis on a face mask, which has been very popular. When the said journalist arrived wearing the face mask, one of the staff asked in surprise, "*Where did you get that mask? I'd really love one!*", explaining that they knew of the painting as "*we've got it here*" suggesting that it is still hanging in its place in the queen's private quarters, where she is still said to "*love it lots*".

On remembering her time back then, becoming a mother, undergoing heartbreak and loss, trusting her instincts, and creating art that people still talk about today – it's a wonder Cindy managed to fit it all in, but she remembers that time of her life with fondness and positivity. Her painting of the corgis has brought so much happiness to many people over the years. Though sad to leave the children at UCH, Cindy affectionately recalls, on numerous occasions, seeing their faces light up when she took out her business cards to show them the brightly coloured painting of the queen's corgis that she had emblazoned across the back of them. Cindy explains,

"Colours are so therapeutic to children and that is why it was such a privilege to paint with them every week. I do miss it."

With these wonderful memories of the UCH children and charmed by the idea that the queen smiles at her painting every day, Cindy can't quite believe everything that has happened to her and all the incredible and inspiring opportunities that have come her way. Cindy explains:

"For most of my life I have learned not to question this path that I'm on but to embrace it, even the bad parts. If the dogs led me to the queen, then it makes me feel that the miscarriage led me to the hospital, where if only for a short period of time, I could help change young people's lives. And I am very grateful for that."

Invitation from The Kennel Club

The Kennel Club (KC) is the oldest recognised kennel club in the world and is dedicated to protecting and promoting the health and welfare of all dogs. Interestingly it also includes The Kennel Club Arts Foundation, a guardian of dog art. Its purpose is to create an archive of important canine artefacts and pieces of dog art and literature, which will co-exist alongside The Kennel Club's current collection.

In 2013, to celebrate the seventy-fifth anniversary of the Welsh Corgi League which first began in 1938, it was decided that with the help of The Kennel Club Arts Foundation and trustee Nick Waters, an exhibition would be held featuring art that depicted these dogs who, at the time, were on the 'At Watch' list of British breeds. These are breeds that number between 300 and 450 registrations, to which the Pembroke Welsh Corgi was added in 2009. Recently in 2018, the Welsh Corgi came off the At Watch list, almost ten-years later, mainly thanks to a resurgence put down in part to the popular Netflix show about the British Royal family, *The Crown*.

And so, canine historian and popular English dog art columnist and photographer Nick Waters began the task of curating an exhibition where most of the art would be leant by Her Majesty the Queen, Patron of the Kennel Club and one of the largest private collectors of Welsh Corgi art. She kindly agreed to lend a collection of paintings and photographs from the Royal Collection for an exhibition, The Welsh Corgi in Art and Literature, which ran from March until July 2015.

One such painting that was missing however, was the work that Cindy did for the Queen. With it residing in her private quarters, it wasn't able to be moved. And so, Nick got in touch on the Kennel Club's behalf. He had previously written about Cindy and commissioned a pawtrait of his own dog where he told Cindy that she had really picked up the character – an amazing compliment. Cindy was incredibly touched by this opportunity, as a huge dog lover she had forged a wonderful relationship with both the Kennel Club in the UK and in the United States. In order to be part of the exhibition, Nick and Cindy gained permission to put together a special lithograph of her artwork, as it was simply too big to be moved.

Once installed. Nick took the time to show Cindy and Jill around the exhibition on its opening day, including both for a tour of the building, stopping for a coffee and explaining how in days gone by, women simply weren't allowed above the first floor in the Kennel Club's offices in Mayfair, London, as it was exclusively men only. While the Club has since moved, a print of the painting *The Queens' Corgis* continues to hang in the gallery. Cindy remembers,

"When I walked into the building, I had to pinch myself when I saw my print among these beautiful, gilded frames. It was just extraordinary to see these amazing portraits from the turn of the century, some 150-years old. It was even more strange to think that just down the road my original was hanging in Buckingham Palace. Nick told me that my painting was among his favourites. When he saw it he fell in love with it. It is the only print to feature in the exhibition of original works and The Kennel Club asked if they could hang it permanently – which is a great honour. My mum was over the moon. She would always say 'reach for the moon and you might touch the stars' and here I was."

CHAPTER 7

CONTINUING HER SUCCESS: CELEBRITY FLOWERS

Flowers Galore

Now that it was two years on from her trip to America, Cindy once again felt a burgeoning need to do something for charity. Invites had flooded in after the press generated by Battersea Dogs Home and DOGNY but while Cindy was happy to donate the odd painting to help a cause she believed in, she felt that a larger showing of her art, driven by some of the celebrity contacts she had made, would make more of a momentous impact to much needed charities. And so, *Celebrity Flowers* began to take shape before debuting in 2006 at the gallery Square One, on New Kings Road in London. Once again, Cindy credits the impetus behind this event to her mother, Jill, who would often beg her to paint flowers. Cindy's thought was that if Jill liked them so much, why not paint the favourite flower of a celebrity and raise money for charity at the same time?

And so, Cindy began reaching out to several A-list celebrities for her next venture, having decided that the project should be geared towards creating awareness and raising money for the Elton John AIDS Foundation (EJAF). In total, Cindy completed fifteen celebrity paintings and added in a few more of her own flowers on square frames that complemented the floral theme.

The Elton John AIDS Foundation (EJAF) is a non-profit organisation established by rock musician Sir Elton John – in 1992 in the United States and 1993 in the United Kingdom – to support innovative HIV prevention, education programs, direct care and support services to people living with HIV. The organisation has raised more than $600 million to support HIV-related programmes in fifty-five countries.

EJAF supports its work through proceeds from special events (just like Cindy's *Celebrity Flowers* exhibition), cause-related marketing projects and voluntary contributions from individuals, corporations and foundations. It is chaired by Sir Elton John's husband, David Furnish, an ex-advertising creative director and producer of theatre and music.

For the Celebrity Flowers exhibition, each of the celebrities nominated their favourite flower, from a simple primrose for Emma Thompson to blood-red roses for Victoria and David Beckham and many other gorgeous blooms. Each of the unique three-feet round flower portraits was further embellished with Swarovski crystals (kindly donated by Nadia Swarovski who upon meeting Cindy in person was absolutely charming and very generous – she simply loved the idea) and signed by the relevant celebrity. Cindy remembers vividly how she created the paintings for the show, persuading powerful women such as Joan Collins,

Emma Thompson and Madonna to take part. To finish the painting and get their seal of approvals, each celebrity then signed their own canvas.

It took a tremendous amount of organisation, but Cindy's *Celebrity Flowers* exhibition took place in London in 2006 at Square One, a venue recommended by Cindy's good friend Ian Monk who had helped secure the IAM's sponsorship for *Celebrity Pawtraits*. He was now heading his own PR firm and suggested the venue which fitted so well the theme that Cindy was trying to create. On the night she wore a neck-turning head piece designed by the floral artists at Moyses Flowers, including fresh flowers from the recent Chelsea Arts show.

The event was covered by leading national newspapers, TV and radio. Flowers chosen by celebrities included:

Sir Elton John (light pink peony)
Madonna (pink English rose)
Victoria and David Beckham (blood-red rose)
Sting and Trudie Styler (dark pink, double-leafed peony)
Paul Bettany (lily)
Emma Thompson (primrose)
Richard O'Brien and Patricia Quinn (sunflower)
Bill Wyman (orange dahlia)
Kylie Minogue (cream gardenia)
George Michael (orchid)
Simon Cowell (white peony)
Liz Hurley (Madonna lily)
Joan Collins (lily-of-the-valley)
Anita Dobson (red amaryllis)
Dame Shirley Bassey (tiger lily)

Celebrities in attendance included guests such as Patricia Quinn and Jackie St Clair. In a nod to the respect that Cindy's art was now gathering across the art community, the forward was by Exhibitions Secretary at The Royal Academy, Norman Rosenthal, who wrote:

> *How fantastic to find a second Flower Show blossoming in the heart of Chelsea. Cindy Lass – self-taught, but no less the artist for that – has been producing her vivaciously coloured, joyous canvases for the last ten years. What is so refreshing is that Cindy herself has no pretensions to producing great art – she simply paints what she feels, straight from the heart.*
>
> *This show allows visitors to see some of Cindy's best work and to enjoy her recent series of Celebrity Flowers, which combine canvas and crystal to heart-jolting effect. Cindy says her only ambition is to make people feel wonderful when looking at her work – I am sure Square One will indeed be full of smiling faces once the magic of Cindy Lass is revealed!*

The show was a phenomenal success with the paintings selling for an average of £5,000 each plus, and all money raised benefitted the Elton John AIDS Foundation. Cindy was ecstatic.

> "I was really thrilled that *Celebrity Flowers* enjoyed such success, but what thrilled me the most was knowing that the sale of the paintings raised both money and awareness for a fantastic cause. On behalf of the Elton John AIDS Foundation (EJAF), I would

like to thank all those celebrities who made time to share their love of flowers and sign their canvases. If the colours in my paintings give a lift to someone's heart, then I feel I have achieved something."

The Beckhams

Two of Cindy's most high-profile clients have been David and Victoria Beckham, whom Cindy contacted via a PA she met at a previous event. Cindy mentioned that she was creating *Celebrity Flowers* and the message was soon passed on to the couple themselves, who volunteered their favourite flowers – and their signatures – for the project. The Elton John Aids Foundation was also close to the couple's hearts as they were friends of the musician themselves.

A message from David was quick to arrive, confirming that his wife, ex-Spice-Girl-turned-fashion-designer Victoria (nicknamed Posh), loved dark red, long-stemmed roses. Only they had to be incredibly long. Cindy set to work. As part of the arrangement, all of the paintings were signed either on the back or the front of the work and the feedback was quick to come in – the Beckhams absolutely loved how Cindy had encrusted the rose with Swarovski crystals. Success!

Kylie Minogue

When Cindy set out to paint the *Celebrity Flowers*, it wasn't just the Queen of Pop – Madonna – that she knew she wanted to enter into the show, but the Princess of Pop also – Kylie

Minogue. While things often have a habit of just happening in Cindy's life, this one needed a bit more planning. Her office first asked Cindy to send in a portfolio and luckily the message came back that Kylie loved her work and would like to take part. After a bit of back and forth over logistics, Cindy then drove over to her London office and left a painting of a gardenia, Kylie's favourite flower, for the *Spinning Around* icon to sign.

While the feedback was that she wanted to keep the flower for herself, Cindy managed to persuade her team that it should go in the show. And although Kylie wasn't able to make it on the night, Cindy made sure it got to her safely afterwards.

Dame Shirley Bassey

Dame Shirley Bassey has always been someone that Cindy admired and what's more, she knew she was a lady that enjoyed a giggle. At one charity event where she was supporting an old friend, actually an old boyfriend who had confided in Cindy that he was gay in their teenage years, Cindy bumped into the *Diamonds are Forever* superstar. Shirley then asked conversationally, "*How come you're here?*" and Cindy replied with a wink, "*Through my friend, I was the girl that made him gay*", which sent Shirley into a fit of laughter. After, Cindy broached the subject of *Celebrity Flowers* and Shirley agreed at once.

When it came to the time to drop the painting off at Shirley's home, Cindy left a note on a card that said,

"Dear Dame Shirley, thank you for your kind support. Hope you like the flower. Please sign the back with a black pen, I will collect it after. Kind regards, Cindy."

And then on the back Cindy asked,

"Please could I have a quote why tiger lily is your favourite flower..." to which Dame Shirley replied:

"I love all lilies, but the tiger lily reminds me of 'Tiger Bay' Cardiff where I was born."

Cindy has kept the note as a permanent reminder of meeting such a talented voice and a brilliant lady.

Dame Joan Collins

Cindy was already good friends with Tara Newley, the daughter of actress Dame Joan Collins – known throughout the world as vengeful schemer Alexis from the *Dynasty* series – and had met her previously at Tara's wedding in 1997. For Cindy, getting Joan on board was a must. Cindy remembers,

"I met Joan at Tara's wedding, she has a great eye for style and knew at once that my white jacket/black skirt combination was Giorgio Armani. Her husband Percy Gibson is absolutely lovely, and Tara is a hugely talented writer. They are all great people, talented and kind."

Cindy went on to paint Joan's favourite flower, lily of the valley, which was then signed and auctioned off for charity.

Richard O'Brien and Patricia Quinn

Any fans of the hit 1980s film the *Rocky Horror Picture Show* will remember actors Richard O'Brien and Patricia Quinn, who played Riff Raff and Magenta respectively (O'Brien not only wrote the original musical but also the adapted screenplay and later became the host of TV gold *The Crystal Maze* for four series).

The pair were both up for getting involved with *Celebrity Flowers* and picked a sunflower, which Cindy was only too happy to present to them for signing over dinner at her house.

It was the most raucous evening – despite never usually asking guests what they thought of her work, Cindy decided to make the exception and ask Richard who simply replied nonchalantly with, "*Yeah it's ok, what do you want me to say?*" but then after setting everyone off with a few giggles, then went on to take the job very seriously and critiqued all of Cindy's work in the house (and he wasn't shy when he didn't like something, but in equal measures, he thought some of Cindy's work was exquisite).

With the easel set up in the dining room, it was quickly decided that he should do some painting, and after producing his own self-portrait, Richard then signed it and presented it to Cindy for her to keep – a memento of a fantastic evening that she still has. Cindy remembers that night for never having laughed so much before and has very fond memories of their glorious meeting. She describes Richard and Patricia as having 'a wicked sense of humour' and still absolutely adores them both.

Paul Bettany

Eventually, the little boy who Cindy would keep company on an afternoon at Corona grew up. She has watched his career progress as he found success in the Marvel Cinematic World. He is well known for his character Vision in *The Avengers*, Dryden Vos in *Solo: A Star Wars Story* and most recently filming alongside actress Claire Foy in *A Very British Scandal*.

For this event, Paul was happy to suggest his favourite flower, a lily, for Cindy to add into the auction. He was also more than happy to provide his signature to aid the sale of the painting on the night. Cindy remembers how utterly charming Paul was when chatting to him for *Celebrity Flowers*. She thinks that he is a very nice guy. Paul was nominated for a BAFTA in 2004 for Best Supporting Actor in his role as Dr Stephen Maturin in *Master and Commander: The Far Side of the World*.

Bill Wyman

While working with celebrities has always been something Cindy has been drawn to, mainly because she treats them just as normal people, she has no one else to oversee the administration. Cindy not only paints but is in charge of sourcing the equipment and canvas needed for the project, arranging individual details with PAs and, in the case of *Celebrity Flowers*, transporting these huge canvases all over London town to have them signed ready for the opening night. It hasn't always left her a lot of time to follow up on feedback of what the celebrities actually thought of their artwork, although she will often hear an anecdote in passing.

One such exception was musician Bill Wyman, bassist for the *Rolling Stones*, for whom Cindy painted a stunning orange dahlia. Certainly, she didn't expect feedback, but Bill got in touch especially to tell her how much he loved it. For Cindy, these unexpected gestures make all the running around worth it, and while this piece was snapped up by another big art collector, Bill told her how much he enjoyed the detail of the piece. Cindy adds:

> "It's funny – when I'm doing a project, I'll have an idea in my mind of what the person is like to work with. And the ones I don't really expect a lot of feedback from, I often get lots. It was so lovely to hear from Bill and I'm glad he liked my work and signed it, with the donation going towards a great cause."

Phillip Schofield

As with any gallery opening or exhibition, Cindy must make sure that not only are her paintings in order, but that she has done all she can to encourage folk to go and look at her work. Not just to buy it but to become inspired and raise awareness

143

of the benefits that colour, painting and crafting in general can bring.

When Cindy was offered the chance to be on Britain's most-loved breakfast show *This Morning* with Fern Britton and Phillip Schofield, she jumped at the chance. Little did she know that the duo wanted not just a tour of her portfolio but a bespoke painting of Phillip's adopted cat, Peaches, a picture of which was hastily couriered over the night before after the producer revealed the bombshell news that she would be painting live on TV.

Already feeling under pressure with just twelve hours to get her head around what this cat looked like, the morning also started with a catastrophe as the promised car was late to arrive, leaving it up to Cindy to get her paints, canvases and stands in by herself. Thanks to a quick taxi, Cindy arrived by the skin of her teeth and managed to set up in the green room before being ferried out to meet the presenting duo. Live and in front of the nation, Cindy showed Fern and Phillip some of her most famous work. These included Dennis and Joseph, Elton John's two dogs.

Fern commented that Cindy's paintings felt very exuberant and asked if she had been trained. Cindy reiterated that she had never had a class in her life but somehow, her first show was a sell-out, and to the viewers, she said that anyone who is passionate about art should give it a go, trained or not.

Moving on to her most recent exhibition, *Celebrity Flowers*. Cindy giggled to Fern that embellishing each painting with Swarovski crystals, kindly gifted by the company, meant that she was forever with terrible nails for a while as the special glue she had to use meant that sometimes she would get a bit mucky.

Then it was time for the *This Morning* hosts to turn the tables on Cindy. Fern jumped in, "*Now we can't have you here without giving you a bit of a challenge. You've told us already it takes six to eight weeks to paint these, how do you feel about fifty minutes?*" Although Cindy had technically already seen the cat, Fern presented her once again with a picture of Phillip's cat, Peaches, who was known as being rather an aloof cat with peachy speckles in her fur. Making sure to accept the challenge on air, Cindy hurried back to her station. The producer followed, asking "*How are you getting on? You're already five minutes late.*" Cindy knew she just had to paint something, anything, despite the print of the cat being as thin as a bus ticket. She tried to tune everyone out and get the paint down onto canvas.

Phillip regularly checked in on her during the show, introducing Cindy as "*the artist who paints the A-lists' mogs and dogs*". He joked, "*Today she's reached the pinnacle of her career – she's painting my cat.*" While Phillip said it was "*looking good*", Cindy playfully wiped her brow wailing, "*I'm having a nervous breakdown!*"

Eventually though, it was time to reveal the pawtrait of Peaches the Schofield puss to the nation. Fern's initial reaction was one of shock: "*Wow look at that!*", whereas Phillip's was more thoughtful. He said, "*Now what you've done here [is] you've given her more of a sense of humour than she's actually got. She's a fairly humourless cat. But that's fantastic.*"

Cindy was pleased with the pair's reaction. She added mischievously:

"That's the Cindy Lass art from the heart canvas 'cause I like to see good in everyone."

Even better, Cindy was able to squeeze in that the upcoming *Celebrity Flowers* show would be taking place at Square One, New Kings Road in London. Amazed at Cindy's quick thinking publicity blitz, Fern turned to her and said, "*You're really good at this aren't you love!*"

Once the cameras stopped rolling, Cindy asked if Phillip would kindly sign the painting and donate it to the Hampstead Hill School, an independent nursery and pre-preparatory school that her children attended at the time. The headmistress, Andrea Taylor, was an amazing woman and Cindy wanted to donate the painting to encourage the children there to enjoy art. Phillip was true to his word and Cindy later kindly dropped it off. She adds,

"All the paintings I have ever done have made some sort of progress to make people smile which has been very important to me. It made me happy that Phillip loved his cat painting and that it was able to inspire a new generation of future artists."

CHAPTER 8

A NEW CHALLENGE: ANNE FRANK

Connecting with Anne Frank

In 2008 shortly after *Celebrity Flowers*, Cindy received two phone calls in the space of a week from friends Ruth Bray and Karen Wootliff, who both wanted her to paint the same thing: the chestnut tree that stood in the garden of Anne Frank's hideaway. It would be to raise funds for the newly developed Anne Frank Trust UK – a tribute to the majestic tree that once gave a teenage girl inspiration and hope during the two years she was concealed from the world. Cindy was blown away by the challenge and determined to help.

She had read Anne's diary when younger and felt like this was a cause she could identify with. What's more, it was going back to her roots in painting, Cindy had painted many trees in her early career; she was captivated by their changing seasons and enjoyed having an artist's control over what part of the tree her paintings would allow people to see – from stark and bare branches to those full of blossom – a tree to Cindy symbolises life. She was incredibly excited to find out more, although little did she realise that this was the start of a journey not just to appreciate Anne and connect with her story, but to understand how our choices as individuals also have impact. Both good and bad.

It was suggested that the artwork be auctioned off at a dinner, but with Cindy's connections, she suggested a private collector in America who was happy to support the charity and prepared to pay $35,000 for this one-off, Cindy Lass artwork. And so, Cindy got to work.

Although she had had a privileged, middle-class upbringing in North London, there were still parts of Anne Frank's story of persecution and racism that Cindy could identify with; she had encountered it many times herself growing up. Aware that what Anne and millions of others experienced continues to this day, Cindy wanted to explore the challenge of painting the chestnut tree outside Anne's window not just as a symbol of persecution, but one of hope that life will get better.

The word 'blossom' was to become pivotal behind the intention of Cindy's painting of the chestnut tree and the message she wanted it to send out to the world.

In *The Diary of a Young Girl* by Anne Frank, the teenager mentions the chestnut tree that stands in the small garden at the back of their hideout on more than one occasion. As the only window not blacked out, she describes how she would often creep up to the attic for a bit of space and time on her own amidst the claustrophobic living quarters and gaze at the patch of blue sky and top of the chestnut tree, witnessing its comparative freedom and the various stages of nature's cycle through the passing of time. At one point in her diary, Anne wrote, "*I firmly believe that nature can bring comfort to all that suffer*", suggesting that the tree must have become a source of solace to her amidst all the uncertainty, horror and chaos that she and her family were experiencing. Anne's father Otto Frank (the only survivor of the eight people hidden away) would later confess to being unaware of Anne's passion for nature, which had not been evident before the war.

> "*How could I have suspected how important the chestnut tree was to her?*" he said. "*But she longed for it during that time when she felt like a caged bird. She only found consolation in thinking about nature.*"

Visiting the Anne Frank Museum

Cindy's first step was to visit the Secret Annex that Anne had spent almost two years inside, along with other families, in an incredibly cramped space at Prinsengracht 263 in Amsterdam. The site used to be a warehouse belonging to her father, Otto Frank, who had built a hiding place for when the Nazis invaded Holland in 1940. In July 1942 the family decided to go into hiding when Anne's sister Margot was called up for 'labour camp', but the four were later taken to Auschwitz when the Secret Annex was found during a raid on the 4th August 1944. In those two years Anne kept a detailed diary, where she described life in the Annex, and the tree featured heavily. The teenager was instructed to keep away from the windows but would often sneak a peek at the tree outside, her only link to the wider world.

In the winter that year, Anne and Margot were moved from Auschwitz to Bergen-Belson, another concentration camp, where they contracted typhoid. By February 1945 they had both died of the disease within days of each other – Anne was just fifteen years old.

When Otto was liberated by the Russians, he returned to Amsterdam, only to find that both his daughters – and also his wife – had perished in the camps. Anne's diary had been saved by friends during the raid, and so in June 1947 Otto made the decision for the world to read what his family had gone through. Honouring Anne's wishes to be heard – and for people to read what she had written. Ten years later, with local residents hearing rumours that it was about to be knocked down, a committee worked with Otto to save the building and preserve the Anne Frank House so that the public could see the effects of the Secret Attic, and learn why Anne's family had to hide away.

When Cindy visited the house in 2009 on a windy morning, she was ushered through the small, dark and bleak hideout where Anne had lived with her family. Looking at the photos of the concentration camp and a video of a woman throwing a parcel over the wall to Anne – the last time she was ever heard from, it made a true impression on Cindy. She said,

"I cried when I left. Being female and Jewish I identified with Anne. My tears were of anger, frustration and sadness for Anne, her family and millions of others. I realised that really it didn't matter whether you were

Jewish or what colour you were, there was hatred around the world. Then there was the tree.

"I had glimpsed it, as Anne once did, from the attic window. I was allowed into the garden next to where this magnificent 150-year-old tree stood. I tried to imagine Anne looking out of the window at it, her despair when then told she could not look – to be seen was just too risky. An occasional peep at night-time was probably all she would be allowed. It has never left me how claustrophobic it felt to be in that room, not able to make a sound inside – a sniffle, a laugh – or even to open a curtain. Simply to exist in the darkness.

"Outside, I was overwhelmed by the number of people queuing, the constant flow of humans honouring this amazing young girl. In this life even a tree will have the chance to blossom, but Anne was never given time to blossom because of her religion, and still to this day, many children miss out because of intolerance and violent hatred. I was desperate to help in my own small way."

Artist's Block – No Time to Blossom

Back in London, Cindy started to think about how she could incorporate all of her thoughts and feelings into painting the chestnut tree. This work of art needed to portray so many different messages and emotions to do it justice. It was a big mountain to climb and a daunting task, perhaps Cindy's most challenging to date.

The first time Cindy sat down in her studio to sketch out the stark, sad-looking chestnut tree, she was overcome with emotion. She felt claustrophobic and couldn't breathe. For three months following Cindy's visit she focused on living in the present. As she walked her dog Ralph every morning after breakfast, she studied the trees on her street for inspiration and insight, but no vision was forthcoming. Never having experienced artist's block for such a long period of time, and with a deadline looming, Cindy felt a little overwhelmed, and decided to take a break from it all. She went skiing with Roger and the boys at the half term in the hope that some distance from the project might allow her a renewed energy for the commission.

Up until that point, Cindy had been focusing on embodying the despair she saw in the desolate, leafless tree; a direct reflection of what she saw and the sadness that surrounded the story. It wasn't until she was on the snow-covered piste – skiing down a beautiful mountain with her family away from her studio and able to let go – that the spirit that guides her as she paints gave her a very strong, clear message. The tree must be painted in blossom. It must be a happy and hopeful image and Cindy immediately knew what it should be called: *Anne Had No Time to Blossom... Everyone Has the Right to Blossom.*

After that revelation, Cindy couldn't wait to get home and start painting. Her artist's block dissipated; the commission suddenly made total sense. She needed to paint the tree full of life and energy. It needed to symbolise the hope that Anne Frank felt when she looked at it each day and bestow the same hope to people viewing it.

One piece from Anne's diary stuck out to Cindy and gave

her the confidence to produce a tree that Anne would have loved to have looked out on. On the 13th May 1944, Anne wrote:

Our chestnut tree is in full bloom. It's covered with leaves and is even more beautiful than last year.

An Important Message from a Friend

Full of renewed energy and inspiration, Cindy set about creating this vision of optimism in her studio. Normally, whilst working on a commission, Cindy wasn't keen on receiving visitors, preferring to ebb and flow as her energy dictated, and create without interruption or outside opinion. However, on this project, a friend of hers who knew and supported what she was doing, Russell Ereira, insisted on seeing the painting one day when he was over at Cindy's house, even before it had been finished. He was pretty dogmatic about it, so Cindy relaxed her usual rules and obliged.

On viewing the unfinished painting, Russell was impressed, but believed that Anne's face had to be included in the painting for it to make sense. Cindy wasn't sure. Portraits were not her forte and she wasn't entirely convinced of the need for its inclusion, but Russell was adamant that the painting must have Anne Frank's face added. Cindy contacted the Anne Frank Trust and asked for their permission to include Anne's face in a photograph among the branches, which was duly granted. Whilst she stood looking at the canvas to see where she should put the face, she was drawn to a specific spot in the blossoming tree's branches.

Russell passed away some years later, and it gives Cindy comfort to know how much he played a part in what was to be one of her most emotional paintings to date.

Bea Klug and Eva Schloss

Once Cindy knew that she would be painting Anne Frank's tree, she started to look for more ways to understand what Anne had gone through. The day she returned from her ski trip Cindy saw an advert for a play about Anne Frank in the West End *And Then They Came for Me: Remembering the World of Anne Frank* at the Phoenix Theatre and decided to buy a ticket to immerse herself fully in her subject matter. That night she met Eva Schloss, Anne Frank's stepsister who, alongside Eva's mother and Anne's father Otto, had also survived the concentration camps and was one of the subjects of the play. Eva also introduced her to Bertha 'Bea' Klug MBE, who was a leading figure for the Anne Frank Trust and a friend of Otto's. She had written a poem: *The Ballad of Anne Frank*. It was here that Cindy promised Bea that when her painting was finished, she would be sure to take it and visit Bea in her home.

And that's exactly what she did a few months later. The pair chatted away in the living room before Bea – who had lost her sight years previously – felt her way around the painting and stopped when she came to Anne's face amongst the branches, enquiring why that part of the canvas felt much smoother than the rest of the painting. On hearing that it was the tiny portrait of Anne, Bea asked Cindy to look at a painting she had of a Japanese tree and to look in exactly the same place in the tree's branches. Cindy duly did as requested and was shocked to see the picture of a man's face peering out from the branches. Bea explained that this was the image of a doctor who had saved her life fifty years ago. Cindy suddenly felt at peace with the painting, that Russell had been right all along, and that Anne was exactly where she was meant to be, radiating peace and hope in the blossom of the tree.

Another fan of the painting was Anita Dobson, who Cindy had confided in many a time before and still remembers with joy when both Anita and her husband, *Queen* guitarist Brian May, asked for a lithograph to hang at home of Anne Frank's tree – both of them thought it was the best work she had ever done and were incredibly moved by it.

Unveiling Anne's Tree with Michael Winner

In order to celebrate what would have been Anne's seventy-ninth birthday on the 12th June 2008, Cindy instigated a plan to plant a tree in her memory. It was also an opportunity to share the finished painting with the public, Cindy decided it would be at a location dear to her heart, at Holland Park. Cindy said at the time:

> "No project has ever been closer to my heart. I have painted this iconic tree in all its beauty, in the hope that all the children of the world can one day be allowed to blossom. I hope the painting keeps alive the image of a tree which gave a glimpse of nature to Anne during her childhood imprisonment and will continue to challenge prejudice, reduce hatred

and raise awareness of what Anne, her family and six million others went through, encouraging the future generation to think about how they treat other people."

When putting together the launch of the painting, Cindy knew that even though this was a much smaller event than she had previously planned, it made good sense to ask for the help of a local celebrity, in order to raise much needed publicity for the Anne Frank Trust. When investigating the neighbours nearby, she landed on an usual name, Sir Michael Winner.

The filmmaker and writer was famed for his unique personality, often giving a scathing critique of some of the more popular establishments. But Cindy remembered him from her school days when she had almost tried out for a part in his film, *The Wicked Lady*. Casting then was undertaken by Hazel Malone, the sister of Miss Rona Knight who had her own agency. When a friend told Cindy that the audition would need to be topless and Cindy refused Hazel replied that *"If you don't go to the audition you're not part of this agency"*. The two then decided to part ways as this was not a path that the young actress wanted to tread despite the potential opportunities.

She met him in person years later at The Halcyon hotel, where on the same night that Cindy's paintings were officially hung, Mick Jagger threw a raucous dinner party and Cindy was invited to join the pre-drinks. Winner was a local who had frequented the restaurant, known as the Room at The Halcyon, during its reign under chef Martin Hadden. But he famously wrote for his column, *Winners Dinners* in *The Sunday Times*, that he would only come back if they fired the chef and "*got rid of those awful paintings that they sell.*" This in part referred to Cindy's own paintings, which decorated the walls during that time. Her friend Larry Adler was furious with him and wrote back to him saying "*Don't diss my lovely artist Cindy Lass*". But when they had met in person, he had been so charming with his quirky sense of humour. Cindy had bumped into him at the bar and he said, "*Did I buy you that dress?*" Cindy replied quickly with a smirk, "*You couldn't afford it*".

Yet these episodes were now years in the past and knowing that he wasn't in great health – he had eaten an oyster in 2007 while on holiday in Barbados, which gave him the rare bacterial infection (Vibrio vulnificus) and was lucky not to have died. His health was now much weaker and he walked with a stick. Cindy got in touch and together they made peace. Cindy says,

> "We all have our own egos and good and bad days. I am so glad he came and helped me unveil my painting on the day, it was so much fun. He could hardly walk but he was a decent guy. It reminded me that I have to learn not to judge so quickly; maybe I would be better at it if I didn't judge myself so much. But I'm getting there."

Emma Thompson

As a participant of *Celebrity Flowers* in 2006, Cindy had already met Academy-award-winning British actress Dame Emma Thompson, known for her roles in *Nanny McPhee*,

Sense and Sensibility and *Love Actually* but also for her work with the Anne Frank Trust.

Emma had spoken passionately about Anne's plight across the world. When launching a new website for the Anne Frank House in 2006, she had movingly said in a speech:

> "The only thing we have to remember is, all her would-haves are our real possibilities. All her would-haves are our opportunities."

During *Celebrity Flowers* the pair had become friends, when Cindy chased the actress around London trying to get her autograph. Emma had agreed to put forward her favourite flower to be recreated as artwork, but the actual event clashed with a filming engagement.

So that she could sign her painting of a primrose ready for the auction, Cindy had to dash down to the set where Emma was currently filming *Last Chance Harvey*. It was here Cindy got her five minutes as a movie star, escorted from one place to the next trying to find Emma during a break in filming. Emma was blown away by the design of her primrose, and happily signed it so that the painting could be put up for auction with her signature. To celebrate, the pair took a photo with the painting next to Emma's trailer. Showbiz indeed!

Emma was naturally interested to see Cindy's new work, featuring the 170-year-old white horse chestnut tree that stood in a neighbouring courtyard. To thank Emma for her work, the Anne Frank House had gifted Emma one of its precious saplings, germinated from some of its last remaining chestnuts. While many were donated to schools named after Anne Frank and other organisations, including the *Amsterdamse Bos* woodland park, others were sent to friends of the House. And Emma was one of them.

Cindy visited her at home with her painting – which Emma absolutely loved. And Emma in turn showed the sapling she had been gifted. Cindy recorded a video of Emma explaining what she had done with the sapling so far. In it she said:

> "This little tree-ling is taken from a cutting that was given to me by the Anne Frank curators when I went to open the website. And it was very small and didn't do very well the first winter. So, we had to put it in the greenhouse. Now it's just doing brilliantly, we're probably going to plant it up in Scotland and hope that as it's a son or daughter of the tree that kept her (Anne) alive, it will keep lots of other people and things alive also."

With similar-aged children, the pair continued to stay in touch and Emma even brought her daughter Gaia over to Cindy's house so that she could do some painting with her sons, Ollie and Jack. It's a fond memory of Cindy's. She said,

> "I just remember hanging out with her and thinking 'wow!' this was a special lady. She was an A-list celeb but would always be so natural and cool. And yet she would give up so much time and donate to good causes. I was really impressed with her as a person.
>
> "I knew she loved primroses, so I painted her another still life after *Celebrity Flowers*. She came over with her daughter to collect it and all the children had great fun painting together. Such a wonderful lady."

Donating to the Anne Frank House

Now that the painting was ready and officially unveiled, it was time to send it across to America so that the Trust could benefit from the raised funds. Eva and Cindy were still good friends and would support the Trust where possible. One day on the way to an event, Eva told Cindy that instead of sending the painting to the private buyer – the painting of which was already secured in its crate due to ship that week – the Anne Frank House in Amsterdam would love to have it. Cindy was overjoyed to hear that her message of hope would now be seen by visitors to the house but a little shocked. The painting was to raise funds for the charity after all – now what would the Trust do? But Eva had a great idea, Cindy could make lithographs of the print and donate one to the Trust and another to the original buyer – which was exactly what she did.

And so, Cindy, alongside Eva Schloss, presented her painting *Everyone Has the Right to Blossom* to the Anne Frank House on the 3rd of May 2010, fifty years after Otto Frank first opened the house to the public. Before going over to Holland for the presentation, Cindy had taken legal advice from a lawyer and decided that instead of gifting the painting she would only loan them the artwork so that it could never be defaced, a small difference which would become very important later on.

Even though Cindy had painted for many celebrities and even the Queen of England herself, on the day she was so moved to be able to put her work into something for the good of mankind itself. She said,

> "The world is sadly still full of racism, intolerance, hatred and anger. For those, like me, who believe

in love, spirituality and the prospect of a better world, the tree symbolises *hope*. And for the sake of our children, *hope* must never be allowed to die. Make this world a better place for us all and for our children's children so that we can *blossom* together."

Anne Frank Tree Sapling

Cindy had already known that the actual chestnut tree outside Prinsengracht 263 that Anne had enjoyed so much had been suffering from disease and was dying. Part of the tree, including its iron construction, had toppled in high winds on the 23rd of August 2010, breaking off at around 1m in height. The remaining trunk was later felled that same year. Fortunately, as she knew by Emma's experience, a number of seedlings of the magnificent tree had been cultivated from its fruit and gifted to various organisations and charities around the world as a message of hope for future generations. What Cindy didn't expect was to be gifted one of the last remaining saplings by the Director at the time. The team at the House were overjoyed with Cindy's kind gift and wanted to repay her by sending her a little piece of Anne's history.

It arrived a few weeks later and after careful thought, Cindy knew exactly where she wanted to plant it: on the grounds of University College School, Hampstead, London, where both her young sons went to school. It was her hope that the children could watch it grow and that it would remind them how fortunate they are to have their freedom.

On Tuesday 22nd March 2011, Eva Schloss, Anne's eighty-one-year-old stepsister, alongside ninety-one year-old Bea

Klug, now an MBE and co-founder of the Anne Frank Trust, joined Cindy on a very moving morning where together they planted the sapling to the sound of a violinist playing the theme song to *Schindler's List*. The tree still thrives there to this day.

Eva Schloss explained to the children at the school how she and Anne Frank were childhood friends who played together from ages eleven to thirteen.

Both families went into hiding separately when the Nazis occupied Amsterdam in 1940 and after being betrayed, they were sent to concentration camps. Her father and brother were murdered as was Anne, her sister Margot, and their mother, Edith. Anne's father, Otto, survived and later married Ms Schloss's mother, Elfriede Geiringer, in 1953.

With Cindy's love of nature – she adores trees – she was honoured to bring her journey with Anne Frank full circle, from trying to help a charity in London raise awareness and stop hate and prejudice, to planting a tree in Anne Frank's memory at the school her own boys went to.

Equally, this new foray into schools gave her something to think about. Both Cindy and Eva took the opportunity to take 'the wisdom of the tree' into schools and encourage children to portray themselves in a painting of a tree, showing the things that made them happy and the things that made them sad. It was the beginning of a new project for Cindy: All Our Hearts Beat As One.

CHAPTER 9

ALL OUR HEARTS BEAT AS ONE

Just like she had experienced a real connection with the children at UCH, Cindy found herself longing to do the same again. But this time she was actively volunteering in schools and sharing her art with them – across London and beyond. For Cindy it felt so satisfying to go into the mixed schools with different cultures. While some would use her art classes to unwind and paint, others were more prone to hold back, and so Cindy thought the best way to encourage them to participate wholeheartedly was to give them the opportunity to have their work displayed in a top London gallery.

Cindy had learned her lesson about promising things that couldn't be achieved. But she knew that she was doing something for the right reason, to develop the artistic and creative talents of young people, so even though she was unsure how this would be achieved, she had hope that an opportunity would present itself. After all, spirit had been kind to her in the past. And as luck would have it, she soon found a gallery who supported the project and was delighted to display the children's work.

Gallery DIFFERENT

It was a day like any other. Cindy was looking through a gallery window while waiting for an appointment in Percy Street. Unexpectedly, a painting with a haunting face on a car door caught her attention. She loved the artist's work and popped in to find out more. It was called Gallery DIFFERENT, and was owned by Karina Phillips, who had recently exchanged a background in law and business to focus instead of contemporary art.

Once Cindy had told Karina her vision – to display the best works of children from various schools in the area, the pair were already talking like old friends. Running late for her appointment, Cindy agreed to come back the next day and talk logistics.

Cindy had already started referring to her work in schools as *All Our Hearts Beat As One*. After everything she had done to raise money for the various charities over the years, Cindy knew that no matter our differences – we were all the same on the inside. What's more, when we worked together, there was a power from our energy that could make things happen. Cindy believes that with our focus in the same direction, e.g., all our hearts beating as one, we really could change the world.

With this to consider, Karina made Cindy a generous offer of giving her the gallery for a week in six months' time. This was the offer of a lifetime; the rents in Fitzrovia at that point were astronomical, and having a 'home' for the competition allowed Cindy to focus on the children and their paintings.

From around three hundred entries, Cindy whittled it down to just thirty finalists. Now all she needed to do was put together an event. The idea was to open the gallery in two parts, to allow friends and family of the children time to come in and explore. Very kindly, actress Jenny Seagrove and Eva Schloss opened it in the morning and Nancy Dell'Olio opened the event in the evening.

All Our Hearts Beat As One, Cindy's mission to create an international day of connection, was launched on 12th September 2012, kindly made possible by the donation of Annabel Schild. Cindy said of the occasion:

> "I invited four schools to participate in the competition by submitting paintings that contained illustrations and words of their feelings. The energy and connection with the lovely Jenny Seagrove opening the show left everyone's heart full of love and understanding that we are all the same.
>
> "I feel touched to have been given such an insight into the strong emotions of these children (whether happy or sad), and I hope that through their artwork, they realise that life is not just about what one can see on the surface, but what is underneath."

The schools that participated were University College School, Quintin Kynaston School, Michael Sobell Sinai School and The Academy School in London.

All Our Hearts Beat As One Celebrity Event

In 2016 Gallery DIFFERENT went on to revive *All Our Hearts Beat As One* with a celebrity event at the same venue. It opened with a VIP Gala event on Thursday 13th October before continuing with an exhibition and other events on Friday 14th and Saturday 15th October 2016.

Cindy knew it was once again time to do something as she became increasingly aware of the effects of depression, mental illness and loneliness. With two young sons now having reached their teenage years, it was easy to see how the ability to communicate directly to individuals all over the world through an increasing number of devices and media had ironically led to more isolation, less personal interaction and a loss of community identity.

She wanted the initiative to help everyone reconnect through the powerful medium of art as a force to 'regenerate' our hearts. Following that theme, she once again turned to her celebrity friends, fifty-five in total from all walks of life – fashion designers, sporting stars, actors, TV personalities and musicians – including Emma Thompson, Bruno Tonioli, Simon Cowell, *Iron Maiden's* Dave Murray and his wife Tamar, Meg Matthews, Melissa Odabash, Mary McCartney, Sinitta and more.

Alongside sixty incredible artists, they each painted their own version of *All Our Hearts Beat As One* on a 20cm x 20cm mini canvas, which were then auctioned at the event with all money raised going to the Heart Cells Foundation, a charity funding a ground-breaking therapy specialising in the physical regeneration of the heart, utilising a patient's own stem cells to treat a range of heart diseases.

This was quite frankly the biggest event Cindy had planned to date and so she was grateful when a chance meeting with an old friend from school led to help with the project, Nikki Newman, an event producer in the entertainment industry, who had been in the year above her at Corona.

One day they bumped into each other and promised to meet up for dinner. Cindy expected to spend an hour catching up but she couldn't tear herself away. Nikki had some heart-breaking news, that she had lost her only child, Sasha (Natasha) Newman, aged just seventeen years old. It led Cindy to explain her own idea to counter loneliness and depression, with a larger version of *All Our Hearts Beat As One*, and Nikki was full of ideas after setting up her own memorial for Sasha – *Peace of Cake day* which takes place every year on her birthday, the 2nd of May. On this day everyone around the world is given the day to remember their loved ones, not just Sasha, by eating the most delicious cake they can find to fill the day with fondness and sweetness, instead of sorrow or loss.

Cindy loved the idea, and Nikki was able to offer all sorts of helpful tips and suggestions to get Cindy's latest idea off the ground with funding and celebrity support, but with her life so hectic in true Cindy style, a few weeks later nothing had yet been done. And so Nikki offered to help – clear that she wasn't to be Cindy's personal assistant – and between Nikki, Karina and Karina's daughter Becky, they helped to co-ordinate the entire show. Following up with artists and celebrities, fundraising, making sure the canvases were back in time, and another of Cindy's friends even set up some meditation and spiritual readings downstairs in the basement, to allow people to take some time out even during the exhibition with the aim that the healing energies would rise up to where the paintings were hung.

On the opening night, Nikki gave a speech about how hard it was to lose Sasha and that now she was keen to impress upon everyone not to sweat the small stuff. And not to stress over families, exams or choice of friends, etc., instead to focus on their health and happiness as that is what matters. Cindy wholeheartedly agreed with Nikki and the pair are still firm friends. Of the event she said,

> "Our emotions make us unique, but if we delve deeper, it's easy to understand that we are one and the same and that all our hearts beat to the same beat. This is the real message I wish to communicate, that we are all so busy looking at one another's differences that we blind ourselves to our similarities.
>
> "I would like to thank my good friend Nikki Newman and Gallery DIFFERENT for allowing me to share my perspective of the world."

Museum of Tolerance

Cindy might have thought that her time with Anne Frank came to a close with the planting of the sapling – but that wasn't the end of the story. In 2013 – following a bitter court battle between The Anne Frank House and The Anne Frank Fonds (an organisation in Switzerland founded by Otto Frank) – a court in Amsterdam awarded the return of some ten thousand photographs and documents that had been loaned to the Anne Frank House. Mercifully, *Anne Had No*

Time to Blossom… Everyone Needs to Blossom wasn't included in the court order as this item was a gift and still belonged to Cindy. Contractually, she had the final say on where her painting was displayed.

Naturally Cindy was starting to think of a new home for her painting. She was still in touch with Eva Schloss, and over a cup of tea Eva told Cindy that the Museum of Tolerance in Los Angeles would be interested in displaying her painting. Cindy couldn't believe it, she had heard many times of the museum from her old friend Russel Ereira and now it seemed as though her life was coming full circle. This suddenly felt right. The Museum of Tolerance (MOT) is the educational arm of the Simon Wiesenthal Center, an internationally renowned Jewish human rights organisation named after a holocaust survivor. The only museum of its kind in the world, the MOT is dedicated to challenging visitors to understand the Holocaust in both historic and contemporary contexts. Cindy's inspiration behind her painting embodied the sadness that Anne Frank was never given time to blossom because she was Jewish and that, still today in the world, there are so many children not given time to blossom because of intolerance and violent hatred. Like Anne, Cindy firmly believes that nature can bring comfort to all that suffer, explaining:

> "I have painted this iconic tree in all its beauty in the hope that all the children of the world can one day be allowed to blossom. I did have a sense that I had been brought onto this planet to put this message across that everyone has the right to blossom. If I died tomorrow, I'd have done something."

The Museum of Tolerance seemed the perfect fit and Cindy arranged for her painting to be shipped to Los Angeles and become part of the museum's immersive exhibit *'Anne'* on the life and legacy of Anne Frank, bringing hope to all and establishing itself as a part of history.

Cindy was invited to give a talk at the museum during an event that was organised to mark what would have been Anne's 90th birthday, but Cindy wanted to do something a little more remarkable. It was her wish that the public on the day could take part in a painting workshop.

The tree she painted and that eventually went to the Anne Frank House was a pivotal moment in her career, where she was able to create a stunning painting that conveyed such a profound message of hope. The journey of the painting itself has been inspirational, from hanging in the Anne Frank House, to being transferred to the Museum of Tolerance, where it formed part of an extensive exhibition on Anne's life and story. The appreciation of museum curators for the piece is testament to how well Cindy captured the sentiment of Anne Frank and her message to the world.

Cindy had a friend who lived in Little Venice, L.A., at the time, the jewellery designer and film producer Carolyn Rodney, whose then partner, now husband, is the filmmaker Steve Bernstein. This meant that instead of having to stay a hotel with all her materials, she could relax with friends. Incidentally, Carolyn was the person who had introduced Cindy to Roger, all those years ago so she would always be a dear friend to her.

Both Carolyn and Steve helped her shop for paints and the three enjoyed a fantastic time catching up before Cindy went on to meet the Museum's director, Liebe Geft. She was warm but formidable; and had invited a mixture of people from different cultures so that Cindy could paint with them. At the heart of the day were six incredibly special holocaust survivors. Cindy was particular taken with Morris Price, who had celebrated his ninetieth birthday just a few months before and still carried a tattoo of the number he had received from the concentration camp where he was sent when just a boy. Cindy says,

"It was just the most amazing day; after I got up to describe the thoughts and feelings I'd had while painting the tree, the survivors all came up to me and thanked me. They were so feisty and wonderful. Then Liebe hugged me and we both started to cry. She told me I'd done a good job. I was in tears once again while talking to Morris, they all had such amazing stories. And then I look over my shoulder and there, at the entrance to the Anne Frank exhibition, is my painting. And it looked exactly like where it was supposed to be. It hit me hard like 'Wow!' but then I realised, it was karma."

Stitch To The Beat

When she was five years old, Cindy loved sewing – it wasn't just the rhythmic stroke of the brush that could bring calm and serenity, it was all types of crafting. Painting was itself a difficult subject to get started with and by nature was a critical and varied space. What's more, materials could be expensive for a beginner. Cindy realised that what was great about needlepoint in particular was that it lent itself to chatting at the same time.

As a busy mum of two, Cindy realised that having an escape like needlework, combined with the opportunity for a chat with like-minded people, would be just the tonic she needed. And if she could benefit, then so could others. Mental health has always been a huge driver for her, and Cindy had previously been involved in the *Snowball Project* where Ollie would play the guitar and friends would make soul food at a gallery belonging to Darren Baker, another Royal artist. Cindy Lass Needlepoint was launched with a similar mindset of bringing people together which eventually led to their first sewing show in 2016 together with Diane Hesford. The pair became good friends and to Cindy's disbelief, they managed to host the show at the famed location Alexandra Palace (Aly Pally).

Working together with healers, sitting in small groups doing needlepoint, the realisation that the rhythm of the group stitching together in time rhymed with a heartbeat inspired the name *Stitch To The Beat*. If *All Our Hearts Beat As One* represents that we're all the same, one of the things we all share is a heartbeat and so, *Stitch To The Beat* was born.

At the Aly Pally show, Cindy was so touched by some of the women she met there. Two of them that she spent time with on needlepoint were the nicest, kindest people she had ever met. Cindy got a different sense from both of them. One of the women couldn't see, and so she was feeling where to stitch with her pinkie finger. Cindy recalls:

"Watching these women really highlighted to me how easy it is to plug into the essence of everything when we're calm and connected. I was so aware of them listening and connecting that to feel so involved made me feel exhausted after just a couple of days of 'stitching to the beat', but I wouldn't have it any other way. There might have been artificial lighting and no fresh air, but I felt like these women put the spark back into my spark plugs. They were so grounded and obviously loved life. The emotion I got from spending so much time with them was very powerful."

After the event, Cindy wanted to raise people's awareness and vibration by connecting people to their hearts through colour. And since she already had a fan base of people who wanted to come to her studio to paint with her, *Stitch To The Beat* was an opportunity to make her art more approachable. Her studio was only so big, after all.

Together with her friends Laraine Krantz and Chrissie Felder, they joined forces and launched the *Stitch To The Beat* needlework. Together they have a desire to spread the activity across Britain, a project the three hope can get women together to do something interesting, yet soothing, to rebalance energies. Cindy is convinced that the project will birth a community where women can take time out of their busy schedule to sit, relax and share.

At this point in her life, she was fascinated by how energy could be used for positivity, and so Cindy created a design using many hands drawn from flags to represent the colours of chakras, previously she decided to use it for *All Our Hearts Beat As One* but now it would also be used for *Stitch To The Beat*. Cindy says:

"This painting is very close to my heart. I painted it to launch *All Our Hearts Beat As One* throughout schools of mixed culture to celebrate each other's differences. The heartbeat is a very important sound and vibration. I hope people will connect through my colourful needlepoint and find an inner peace whilst stitching, feeling the love for oneself and others."

During the lockdowns, people have been so appreciative of Cindy's needlepoint designs; one friend who she went to Corona with said that through the first lockdown, her mother had completed each of the nine designs currently available. For her, this was more than a feeling of achievement – it had saved her from loneliness and despair.

Each of the paintings has a story. Each has its own energy. Her goal is for our hearts to beat as one and together, to 'stitch to the beat'.

The current situation of a global pandemic has brought Cindy a lot of anxiety. She cares deeply that so many people are affected and that so many lives will have changed forever. However, for the first time in decades, Cindy is not racing to do a show or a charity event. She is finally able to enjoy the one thing that has eluded her for far too long a time. Her entire adult life she has been relentlessly busy, trying to fit everything in and has neglected to take care of her own emotions, never setting herself boundaries.

Over time, Cindy has come to realise she is an empath. She is highly aware of other people's feelings. If someone is upset in a room, she feels that energy tenfold. And now, with time, she is finally learning to help others without letting their emotions weigh her down.

Part of her journey with this new awareness has been accepting that she can't be at her full capacity all of the time, and that's okay. Whether she's in a good mood or not, painting has always been her refuge.

CHAPTER 10

ALMOST LOSING HER FATHER

Preparing for the News

In January 1995, Cindy received the most harrowing news she'd ever had to deal with. Her father had developed a blood clot which had travelled to his neck. He had been admitted to Middlesex Hospital and would be undergoing a delicate operation the following day. Given her father's condition, the doctor told Cindy that he had a fifty-fifty chance of suffering a heart attack and therefore, survival.

With a heavy heart, scared and completely overwhelmed, she sat in the hospital's stairway, howling and crying without the slightest idea of what to do next. Her siblings, Tracy and Craig, were wrapped up in the hustle and bustle of life. To make matters even more unbearable, the news of her father came when Jill, with whom she would normally speak with multiple times a day, had been on a cruise for the last few weeks, meaning it was virtually impossible to get in touch. For the first time in her life Cindy could no longer call Jill freely – she was completely lost.

The Nurse That Opened Up

And so, she found herself on the way to hospital, alone. Cindy remembers sitting on the stairway, hearing someone crying but not realising that the noise was coming from herself, when a nurse sat down beside her. Cindy noticed (as her uniform was slightly open) that she had a huge scar on her neck and chest. Kindly, the nurse asked her why she was sobbing. Holding back the tears, Cindy mumbled the news, that she thought her father was dying and that she didn't know what to do.

Calmly, the nurse told her something she would never forget. She told her that if her father survived, she had to be strong to take care of him, and if he didn't, she still needed to look after herself and her family. Years later, Cindy would think on how the nurse's words rang true. Despite being the youngest, she had to be the one to take care of her siblings as they were not ready to let go of their father when he died. Through her conversation with this nurse, she mustered the courage to soldier on from that day forward.

Alongside the good advice, Cindy drew strength from a personal story the nurse shared with her. The nurse had elderly parents and two young children when she met a lovely man with whom she hoped to build a life with. Convinced that it was the right thing to do, she took the plunge and moved abroad with her parents and every penny they owned

– a decision that she regretted later but refused to let define her.

While she was working hard and settling everyone in, she discovered that she had cancer. Despite the sad news, she trusted that despite the circumstances, the new man in her life would take care of her young children. Instead, he did the unthinkable. He cleared out their joint bank account and did a runner. Despite the betrayal, the nurse got better with time, managed to find money to fly her parents and her children home and started all over again. She said she had no time to play the victim.

It gave Cindy a moment of perspective to realise that hers was not an insurmountable problem, so she dried her tears and somehow found the strength to drive home. But now she was home, what else could she do but wait for a phone call from the hospital? Beside herself, Cindy pushed a shepherd's pie from Marks and Spencer in the oven, then made the decision to get out her paints.

Pointillism

At the time, she lived in a ground floor flat with a lovely kitchen facing a beautiful garden that they were not allowed access to. As a young couple, Cindy and Roger were forever locked out of an oasis. To say this was frustrating is an understatement. It was infuriating. The garden was so beautiful, beckoning her to step in and explore, yet she couldn't. So, she submerged herself in painting to stay sane. Armed with a bag of acrylic paints, she started sketching the front and back of the garden.

When she had first met Barbara Grundy at Ebury Street Gallery, the painting of the blue vase was a water colour. Barbara had mentioned that at some point she should try acrylic. With time stretching ahead of her, Cindy got out her paints and dived in. Only this paint was drastically different, it dried instantly on the brush and Cindy found herself constantly wiping off the excess. In the end she resorted to dipping the end of the brush in the paint and 'dotting' her way around the canvas.

Unbeknownst to Cindy, she was actually using a technique called pointillism (in which small, distinct dots of colour are applied in patterns to form an image. Developed by Georges Seurat and Paul Signac in 1886, it was a branch of art stretching from Impressionism).

Back then, Cindy didn't have the slightest idea about this technique. It was her first time using acrylic and at that moment, Cindy found it a way to quell her need to paint, distressed as she was. When each of the brushes quickly dried up, it left her with no option but to dot the paint onto the canvas.

What Cindy didn't know was that acrylic dried very quickly and that she needed to use retarder to make it stay moist, something that Barbara failed to pass on in the short conversation they had had on acrylics. Her paintbrush might have felt like a screwdriver, but that didn't stop her.

Ten brushes down and hours of hard work later, Cindy produced two masterpieces: '*The Secret Garden*' (focusing on the back of the garden that was forbidden) and '*The Bench*' (focusing on the front of the house – the bench used to sit neatly next to Cindy's basement entrance). '*The Bench*' was a symbol of stability at a time when everything else around her was falling apart. It took her months as she tried to polish the lines and add a bit of an artistic twist to make the bench appear full of sunshine.

Cindy admits that she had never painted a scene in either acrylic or watercolour like that before, and neither has she done it again since. These paintings are part of her collection that she can never sell. Although the paintings were once sold in her first show, she repurchased them, distraught with herself that they were in the company of someone else who didn't understand the emotion behind the art. To this day, Cindy is so relieved that she got those paintings back, because they were incredibly special to her, full of sentimental value. They saved her when she was home alone as her father lay in hospital.

Throughout her career, Cindy has never really looked at another artist's work. Everything she does is self-taught and comes from her heart. She does, however, draw inspiration from artists such as Beryl Cook, a well-known artist who was also self-taught just like her. Jill later went on to live opposite to British painter Lucian Freud and the pair bumped into each other at The Wolesley restaurant one day, Jill asked if he would paint Cindy. He immediately said yes and told Cindy to contact him to name the date, but as with most things, life got in the way. One of Cindy's biggest regrets was that she never got back in touch with him, as he died in 2011.

Saying Goodbye to Jack

As her father recovered, Cindy continued to paint many more pictures in her kitchen. It became her therapy and way of coping, painting non-stop until her father recovered.

But more health complications arose. While he enjoyed almost two decades more of good health, eventually Jack developed angina and then dementia, which meant he had to be moved to a care home. Within a couple of years, he had developed a multitude of complications, including diabetes, and died.

When the time came it was less of a surprise, but Cindy still remembered the wise words of the nurse in hospital. She shouldered her sibling's grief, now able to talk through her concerns with Jill. Cindy says,

> "It was so sad to see this handsome, charismatic, amazing man that started his own company aged fourteen and looked after all of his brothers and sisters, go downhill. But as my Mum would say to me, he had lived a very full and wonderful life.
>
> "He was the first man in Hampstead to own his own international bespoke car with beautiful red leather seats, he was a self-made, wealthy individual that built the house of his dreams on The Bishops Avenue. But most of all he was a kind, generous and wonderful man."

The one piece of advice she still remembers from Jack – even now, fifteen-plus years after his death – is that as long as she has self-respect, she can walk into any room around the world with her head held high.

Cindy asserts that through the years, she came to understand that we are here to find our purpose, and this might mean that spirit will test us until they know we are strong enough.

Painting Over

The key thing to really understand when it comes to Cindy is that life without art and the ability to paint is simply no life at all. When she goes without painting for long periods of time, she likens it to not being able to breath. But there were times in the younger days of her marriage when paints and canvas had to be prioritised as they didn't have enough space or resources to feed Cindy's hunger to paint.

Only once has Cindy ever painted over an earlier design. She took a dislike to an old painting of two fishes and painted a bright red strawberry with yellow seeds over the top which an art collector went on to buy.

It was a mixed experience for Cindy and something she's not keen to repeat. In a way, she feels a loss from the earlier fish painting, despite being able to then paint something she liked more over the top. From then on, she's always found space to house her art around whichever house she has lived in over the years. Her painting space stopped being a whim and became a need instead, whether it was the conservatory in the early years or now her own office. Cindy is in control of her own artistic needs.

CHAPTER 11

BRINGING BACK HER UNCLE

The Crystal

Late one morning in 2015, Cindy received a phone call from her mother Jill to say that her uncle, then aged eighty-five, was in the King Edward VII's hospital on Beaumont Street in London after falling out of bed. Cindy went to visit, a difficult task as she wasn't great with hospitals after her previous experiences, but this time, something strange happened.

On her way out of the house Cindy picked up the usual – handbag, keys, mobile phone. But it felt like she was missing something; not really understanding what it could be, she ran back in and grabbed a quartz crystal that had sat in her office since she was gifted it by an amazing woman that Cindy knew to be a healer.

Her friend Laraine had introduced her to a circle of twenty like-minded and very powerful ladies who were open to the energy and spirit in the room. While Cindy was only at the beginning of her journey into exploring the power of human connection, one of the women brought out a box of crystals and said, "*help yourself*". Cindy was drawn to a long, tall crystal made of quartz but had never really felt a need to use it. And so it had sat on a shelf in her office gathering dust. Until now.

Cindy arrived expecting to see her aunt and cousin, hoping to stay for a short while before meeting up with Roger for a planned lunch. But the room was empty; it looked as though whoever had been there was taking a short break. On first glance, things didn't look good, unbeknown to Cindy, her uncle had had a cardiac arrest. His eyes were closed, his skin was sallow, and sound of the beeping monitors was deafening. Cindy nearly didn't go in because he looked so grey – she was worried he was about to die. But without knowing where she found such an attitude, she purposely strode into the room and took his cold hand.

Vaguely, she knew that quartz crystals had healing powers, but she had never looked much further into it. Cindy made it so that her uncle was holding the crystal, which was difficult as it was bulky, and his hands weren't able to grip. Cindy was concerned that if he rolled over, he might cut his skin, even though most of the edges were smooth. As she was considering how to make sure that it was left in a good way, a nurse ran in, scaring Cindy by shouting about how she shouldn't try and wake him up.

Cindy hadn't realised but he had been put in a medically induced coma so that his body could focus on repairing its organs rather than regulating, a risky procedure for a man of his advanced years and so the prognosis was bleak. The question was, would he survive? And if so, would he ever be the same again?

Once Cindy had explained that she wasn't trying to wake him, she just felt that he should have the crystal, the nurse calmed down. She told her to sit down next to him and talk to him, that he might be able to hear her. Knowing she'd be late for lunch if she stayed much longer, Cindy was about to make her apologies and ask the nurse to look after the crystal so that her uncle wasn't hurt, but something make her sit down.

Back at Brighton Beach

The noises of the machines started to fade and Cindy found herself hearing waves, closely followed by the noise of seagulls. She wondered what to talk about. Usually, he would be quite chatty and in the mood to talk, known as quite a character. Yet in this environment, faking a happy conversation was the last thing Cindy wanted to do. But as Cindy closed her eyes, sat in the hospital chair, she found it wasn't just the waves she could hear, now she could smell the sea air and, even better, fish and chips!

With her eyes still closed, everything suddenly switched on as if she was in the daylight at the seaside – standing next to her, she saw her uncle. He put his arm in hers and they began strolling down small streets Cindy hadn't been to since she was a small girl. She recognised them as the Brighton lanes. They looked in colourful shop windows and followed their nose to the fish and chip stall, finding a bench to sit on and eat them while watching the waves roll in over the sea.

She continued her daydream, recalling the sights and smells of Brighton as they walked.

Eventually, Cindy came to and realised how late she was, as she looked down she could see a little colour had returned to his cheeks. On her way out she met her aunt, coming out of the visitor's room and made sure to tell her not to remove the crystal, she just had a feeling he was meant to have it.

Good News

As Cindy got further away from the hospital, she began to feel more like herself. So, when Jill rang a few hours later she had almost forgotten her experience that morning. Cindy remembers,

> "I picked up the phone and I heard my mother's voice yell '*What did you do to him?*'. It's funny how quickly you can find yourself in the past. Hearing her tone of voice, I was immediately transported back to being a little girl when she was cross with me and feeling like I needed to hide or run away. My heart sank, and I felt awful hoping that the crystal hadn't harmed my uncle."

But it turned out that Jill had good news, whatever Cindy had done, just a few hours later her uncle was sat up and talking with the hospital who said he would be able to return home in a few days. But Jill had a question: how had Cindy known that he had spent his youth in Brighton?

Cindy was confused, she wasn't aware at all that her uncle had spent time in Brighton, but somehow that day she knew she had to talk to him about it. He obviously needed to hear her chat away about strolling through the arcade and how good the fish and chips tasted. To the rest of the family it was an absolute miracle, but Cindy didn't quite feel like celebrating. It would be like taking credit for something she didn't do. Cindy says,

> "To this day, it's something that the family rarely talks about. Yet for my uncle, he carries the crystal with him wherever he goes, even just from room to room. But a few years later when we celebrated my mother's birthday in his favourite restaurant, Claridge's, where he was well known, the maître d' said to me *'you're the niece who saved his life'*.
>
> "So, I think he is more thankful than I realised, and since the experience, I find myself quietly healing wherever I can."

CHAPTER 12

THE ROLE OF SPIRITUALITY

Understanding Spirit

For many people there will come a time in their lives when the thoughts and feelings they encounter seem to come from nowhere. You might think "*Why did I say that?*" or "*What made me act that way?*" and for Cindy she has found that as long as she doesn't question it, then this spirit can be a positive force in her life.

Painting has only made this feeling stronger, and now there are times when the urge to paint is as strong as the urge to eat. What's more, Cindy often finds a long way down the line, why there was a sudden urge to paint. Perhaps the painting connected her with a person she was supposed to speak to, or it sold and raised large amounts of money for charity.

Over the years, Cindy has explored some of the ways in which she can channel the spirit, some which have worked better than others. Like with her uncle, she knows that there are ways to use crystals for positive energy to heal – tapping into *All Our Hearts Beat As One*, Cindy feels that we all carry a vibration and some of us are kindred spirits – we live life on the same frequency.

But one of the dangers of opening yourself up to a force that guides you is that it can pivot and open up new channels that you had never thought to explore previously. And this knowledge can be a burden, where pain and grief, even which belongs to someone else, can often resonate more keenly.

Putting paint on canvas is the only time Cindy is able to switch off; when her incredibly busy mind is put on standby, creativity can truly flow and she can enter an almost trance-like state, enabling her spirit – who she likes to think of as a 'wise old man' – to take over. Cindy candidly reveals:

> "I thrive off the energy that painting creates; when you look at my work you see my soul stripped bare. Most people wouldn't want you to see that, but I want to share my soul with the world as painting is the only time I can fully be myself. Not a wife or a mother, just Cindy."

Recognising this is how she works best, Cindy is unfazed when she gets artist's block, as every artist does and as happened when she was creating her Anne Frank piece. Instead, she waits for a message of what to do next. It could come in a nod from a robin on a cold morning, seeing a beautiful sunrise over a rolling sea, or lying awake in bed and listening to the wind howl around her. Before long, she will be putting brush to canvas and instinctively know what to do next.

Champagne and Santorini

'Spirit doesn't work with ego' is somewhat of a motto for Cindy, which is evident by the way she lives her life, making sure she goes out of her way to help those she can. Whilst holidaying in Santorini one year, Cindy saw a woman; she looked upset and dishevelled.

Something changed in Cindy's mind's eye, and she began to feel the pain this woman was going through, slumped up against the wall of the hotel. Cindy didn't want to offend her but approached gently – realising quickly that she was only sad and having a bad day rather than physically hurt, a solution suddenly came to mind. Without thinking twice, she raced up three flights of stairs to get the bottle of champagne and generous food the hotel had left in her room and brought it to the woman. The couple were leaving the next day and something told Cindy to trek all the way back up those famous Santorini steps to grab them. In shock, the woman listened as Cindy told her how she somehow understood just what this person had been through – and that it was a lot to bear, but even so, she hadn't let it embitter her. Cindy wanted to leave the poor woman with encouragement – hence the food and drink. She just needed to keep going.

It seemed to be just what she needed to hear, collapsing into floods of tears, telling Cindy her life story and confessing that she just needed someone to notice her. With that one moment, Cindy had engineered a little ray of light and added kindness into her life at a crucial point. A small gesture with a big impact, brought about through empathy, insight and awareness of others.

The Girls' Holiday That Almost Never Was

Cindy's gift helped another friend in need when they experienced a medical emergency. Cindy was good friends with Tamar Murray, (wife of Dave Murray, guitarist in rock group *Iron Maiden*), who Cindy first met at the tennis club. She finds it funny that two of her good friends, Tamar and Anita Dobson, are married to men who are both amazing lead guitarists in rock music (*Iron Maiden* and *Queen* respectively), but they are actually married to two of the sweetest men alive. 'Gentle souls', she calls them.

She had finally found the time in her diary to join Tamar on a girls' weekend in Nashville when one of the women in the group who suffered from a rare brittle bone condition, was rushed to hospital in agony. She had slipped in the restaurant, completely shattering her shoulder. The following morning, Cindy and Tamar went to visit their friend in the hospital, only to find her still on a trolley in the corridor in great pain, waiting for paperwork to be signed off so she could have an operation. This was bad news, as the whole group were due to fly to Las Vegas tomorrow and this couldn't happen without the final guest. Everyone back at the hotel was hoping there would be good news.

The poor lady was trembling after being left out on a cold trolley, so Cindy went to calm her. She placed her hands a couple of inches away from her shoulder and, fifteen minutes later, she was able to sleep, the pain had reduced so much. An hour after Cindy left the hospital, the friend rang in amazement to say that, following a second X-ray, the injury had miraculously healed itself and she would be allowed to fly the next morning! To this day, the lady still refers to Cindy as

'God' thanks to the healing power she demonstrated. As for Cindy, she doesn't dwell on it too much but knows that there is strength in numbers; a lot of people were hoping for the woman to get better after all.

While Cindy is also pragmatic, she acknowledges that intent is a very powerful thing. She has heard many anecdotes that recall moments, post talking to her, that have changed lives in positive ways.

Action on Addiction

For Cindy, it's not just the calm of the paintings that she enjoys. It's the glitz and the glam that go alongside the promo of a painting or an exhibition. Cindy says:

> "I'd be a liar if I didn't say I get a kick out of the marketing – I enjoy marketing. From gallery openings to meeting people."

During her gallery openings, Cindy was meeting a lot of people and not all of them had good intentions. One such person offered her a contract with a car company, but while the offer was a good one – and the money would have benefited a family with two small children – something seemed wrong to Cindy. Put simply, she didn't like their energy.

While there could have been many times that Cindy had her name in lights or a bulging bank account, she feels at peace that this is the path she chose. There was one occasion where through a friend, Cindy had met a woman that wanted to use Cindy's dogs and flowers on greeting cards that would be available for sale around the world. But on meeting with the woman, Cindy found her brusque, and she didn't feel as though she would be able to communicate well with her; certainly they wouldn't be able to talk as friends.

This sort of relationship (a vibration as Cindy would call it) is something that is incredibly important to her, much more than money. While Cindy took the contract to a lawyer who said it was very good and the woman apologised afterwards and said she had an ill family member, it wasn't enough to get the spark back. Lots of people wanted to cash in on the Cindy Lass brand but Cindy has never progressed unless it felt right. However, the urge to do something big was still there. Knowing that Action on Addiction were looking for something to get behind, Cindy on a whim went into ASK pizza in Hampstead and before long they had joined forces. Cindy loves working as a team and the ones at both ASK and Action on Addiction were phenomenal and Cindy was so pleased to work with them.

She put forward a plan where she would lend her *Celebrity Pawtraits* paintings to the company in return for a charity donation to Action on Addiction, a UK-based charity ran by Lesley King-Lewis that was dear to Cindy's heart. It worked with people affected by drug and alcohol addiction, and the chain were happy to oblige. They used the image of Charlie Sheen's pug dog, Hank, on the Florentine pizza where for every sale, twenty-five pence went to the charity. What's more, children dining at the restaurants were asked to submit their own drawings which Cindy got to judge. She says:

"It meant I got to go up and down England doing an art competition and meeting all these kids. I really enjoyed it; it's one of the best things I've ever done. It was a great success, and we found a winner who even had his art printed on the front of a pizza box."

Action on Addiction now counts the Duchess of Cambridge as patron of its charity.

While able to choose an overall winner, the restaurant chain also suggested smaller winners for various age categories – a tough responsibility for Cindy as in truth, she felt they had all done so well.

Seeing the children so happy with their painting only spurred Cindy on to get back to her own oasis. The conservatory was where Cindy found her peace and quiet to paint. Whether she was happy or stressed, when she walked in the room it was like tuning the dial on a radio station. Her brain simply stopped thinking, her hands grabbed the brushes and she just painted. Bliss. Being calm and focused allows Cindy to contemplate higher matters.

Over the years, Cindy has felt many urges to pass on messages to people. Once, in a restaurant, she felt compelled to tell the waiter that it was not his fault he was abused as a child. They both burst into tears, so moved by the experience. Luckily, her newfound friend singer-songwriter Heather Nova was there to guide her through such an experience and has been a guiding light since. However, Cindy's gift isn't always initially appreciated and on occasion, the phrase 'don't shoot the messenger' springs to mind.

Bad Energy at Gallery DIFFERENT

One of Cindy's success stories, *All Our Hearts Beat As One*, was the celebrity edition in 2016 which featured fifty-five hearts in squares painted by celebrities. It showcased at Gallery DIFFERENT on Percy Street in London, but almost didn't happen due to the spirit in Cindy's life.

Karina was once again delighted to host Cindy's latest project at the gallery. Two weeks before the opening, Cindy arrived at the venue to see how things were taking shape. She was immediately struck by a blockage; a feeling that all was not well with the building's aura and – not one to mince her words – announced, "*The energy here is blocked.*" This revelation was met with such great upset by Karina that Cindy thought it better to leave and try to sort it out the next day.

Feeling utterly distraught at her bluntness causing so much upset, Cindy begged her friend Nikki to help with a chance to explain, but they both agreed to leave it a few days. Eventually, she managed to meet up with Karina's husband at a little Greek Taverna next to the gallery for a coffee and the chance to redeem herself, or at least explain. Karina's husband admitted that, whilst he wasn't one to believe in the spiritual side of things or understand different energy flows, his wife had felt there was something not quite right at the gallery and hearing Cindy verbalise the same intuition as soon as she set foot inside the door scared her.

Cindy explained that negative energy can be caused by lots of things, some as simple as positioning tables and chairs incorrectly (feng shui). Karina's husband asked what they could do to rectify the problem and whether it could be done in time for the exhibition in three days' time.

Remembering how they had helped her uncle, Cindy instantly recommended crystals, and she worked with Nikki to get hold of a powerful crystal grid ran by Talia Santo that would help clear the area. Whether it was the crystals, the furniture or just Cindy's intuition, the exhibition went on to be a great success.

Perhaps because of incidents like these, Cindy is more careful in the messages and hints she gives out to people. But Cindy is keenly aware how being receptive to energy and spirit has helped her face the many obstacles the universe has placed in her way, both in her personal life and in art. Whilst working on large-scale projects, including the pawtraits series and Anne Frank's tree, she has come to understand that the obstacles she faces are all part of the process and that she must trust her guide and intuition to do the work for her.

Cindy the Healer

The craziest things seem to happen to Cindy on nights out to places she doesn't want to go. Back in the early 2000s, Cindy often had an invite to whatever event was taking place in central London. On one night, prestigious *OK! Magazine* had an event at Tokyo Joes, a lounge by day and private members nightclub in the early hours. Cindy already knew the magazine owner Richard Desmond as he used to give her sister Tracy a lift after work on Saturdays when they lived in White Lodge Close. Tracy used to work in the White Rabbit record shop in Wood Green which Richard owned, and so he would often drop her back home afterwards, mentioning that one day he wanted to live in White Lodge Close also – something he did eventually achieve although has since moved on.

This night Cindy's date was Patricia Quinn, most well-known for her role as Magenta in the 1975 film *The Rocky Horror Picture Show* and also technically Lady Stephens, as she had inherited her late husband's title. Cindy was at this point worried about her dad, Jack, and so wasn't sure she should attend such an event but she knew she always felt better after a good night out.

Despite her initial reluctance, the pair had a great night as Patricia is fantastic company, but on their way out the door they spotted Anton Bilton, a property entrepreneur. Cindy was drawn to him and after saying hello she said, "*You look like an old soul.*" He was surprised as someone else had also said that to him the same day – a healer by the name of Amaryllis Fraser. Cindy knew that this was a sign she had to meet her and so asked for her contact details. Anton gladly gave them, but suggested before she went, Cindy should write on a piece of paper who she would like to contact.

Once she had arranged to go and see Amaryllis, Cindy's dad was unfortunately back in hospital. Although this was years after his experience with the blood clot, he was now suffering from dementia and other complications; the family knew it wouldn't be long. Still, Roger was determined that his wife should follow her instincts, soothing her by telling her that Jack would be here a little while longer. She went to see Jack before the appointment with the idea that perhaps she could try and massage his feet to give him a bit of comfort. He had pulled out his drip and looked dreadfully ill. But he was so bruised and his feet were wrapped up in the sheets that she gave it a miss, with the intent to try again the next day.

Cindy went on to see the healer, parking in Portobello Road and then knocked on the door, where to her surprise a stunning and gorgeous young woman with a floppy hat opened the door. Cindy wasn't sure what to expect, an old woman perhaps? She was surprised to see someone so young. At that point, Cindy had had little experience with healing apart from her brush with crystals, but was happy to see if Amaryllis could help her contact some of the loved ones she had lost, such as her grandmother on Jill's side, as well as her Larry Adler. Almost immediately Larry seemed to come through. Amaryllis had said, "*Oh there's lots of famous people around this old man*" which was the wrong thing to say – Larry hated to be called old, and he made sure to let them know that he was mad about it.

As they sat opposite each other, Cindy's grandmother also seemed to appear with the news that she had Jill's twin brother by her legs. This was something that gave Cindy a feeling of peace, as Jill never really wanted to talk about the fact that she was a twin, her brother Gary had died aged 3-months old, but it was certainly something the rest of the family had never discussed. After researching, Cindy found that Gary was probably a victim of cot death before it was known such a condition existed and in shame, Jill's mother had simply never talked about it, fearing she was somehow at fault. In a way, this made so much sense to Cindy and her family. While Jill was supportive of Cindy's efforts, there were many times when the pair didn't get on and it was almost as though Jill was lost and looking for something – or somebody. Perhaps she was meant to have a twin brother by her side all along.

Understanding as she does the power of colour it is perhaps no coincidence that Amaryllis has gone on in her career to produce stunning art that incorporates healing powers. Cindy felt that day that so much in life is unexplained, but as long as she accepted it without questioning it, she could use her art for the benefit of so many others. Something that Amaryllis has also expanded upon, and the pair still keep in contact via social media.

The next day Cindy returned to the hospital with lavender oil, determined that nothing would stop her from trying to help her dad. She found his feet in the same state, unwrapped the sheets and performed. As time went on, Jack's breathing changed from short rattles to deep, peaceful breaths. That was the last time Cindy was able to touch Jack and two days later he died. Suddenly it made sense, Amaryllis passed on the message that Larry kept saying 'feet'. Little did Cindy know that this was an instruction and it was only later that she realised that it would help her poor dad pass much quicker. Cindy says,

"I feel so blessed that I was able to spend that time with him, but looking back at that trip to Amaryllis, there was definitely a sign from Larry that he was going to look after my dad. He had a habit of always ringing me to see how I was when I was passing through Hampstead going back to St John's Wood. It always was the journey coming back from seeing my father. I feel like the pair were meant to be connected."

Comfort on Primrose Hill

Cindy loves to take photographs of nature to inspire her when she is painting. These trips are often spontaneous and one morning she felt like walking in Primrose Hill to take pictures of the trees. Up ahead on the hill was a little boy of around eight years old wearing a jogging suit, who was walking with a lady that Cindy assumed to be his mother and a little shaggy dog. As Cindy pointed the camera at one of the trees above them, she heard her call out not to take their picture. Cindy explained that she was an artist and that she wasn't taking pictures of them and the woman apologised by explaining that she wasn't actually the boy's mother, but a neighbour. The poor child had had a traumatic day; his dog had been run over and he was worried whether or not it would pull through.

Cindy stopped and suggested that the boy come with her to a nearby tree and give it a cuddle. She asked the boy to tell her all about the dog and what it looked like, trying to really focus on the dog healing, ending by saying that if he went to school he would come home and the dog would be better.

Once they had said goodbye Cindy visualised the dog getting better from the description she had been given. She got a bit emotional but was able to push the thoughts away. A few days later on a different place on the hill, Cindy came across a woman on the phone who started waving at her. She heard her say "*I'll have to call you back*" and rushed over to remind her that she was the neighbour of the little boy. Miraculously, the dog had made a full recovery and the child was convinced it was all Cindy's doing. Of course, Cindy hadn't clicked that it was the same lady without the young boy and while once again she struggled to explain how she knew the dog would be ok, Cindy believes the universe is an amazing place.

The Photographer in Dublin

During her career, Cindy has received countless invitations to exhibit. She was once kindly invited to hang her art in an exhibition in Dublin by Maureen and Laurence Benezra. Cindy was to be a guest and meet Doreen Smurfit whose family owned a large art collection by Irish artists. The exhibition was charming but during the day, Cindy found herself drawn to the photographer at the event. She felt like she knew so much about his history; he was also from London and they talked about his little girl and other ambitions.

The pair had a deep talk about very personal experiences and he decided that he needed to leave the event. It now seemed clear to him what his future purpose was. The only problem was that Cindy now had to explain what had happened to the photographer; her hosts were only barely halfway through the event and Cindy was yet to meet special guest Doreen. Cindy got the feeling that the organisers weren't best pleased with her after that.

Brahma Kumaris

Cindy often finds herself making new friends wherever she goes. One family holiday in Marbella while the boys were young, she was delighted to meet a couple, Jayne and

George Dionysius. George later became great friends with Roger introducing him to meditation. They also lived in St John's Wood in London. They grew close over the years and through Roger, the couple helped them develop a burgeoning interest in spirituality. Things just seemed to happen to Cindy and she wanted to find out if there was a way to control or influence them, even if she couldn't understand them. The pair recommended that Cindy and Roger look into a spiritual organisation called Brahma Kumaris, as it was great for meditation and they had much enjoyed their own experience. The group philosophy of Brahma Kumaris is that our true identity is not the physical form but the spiritual being that embodies love, peace, purity and understanding, which seemed to fit seamlessly with Cindy's views and beliefs.

Roger and Cindy then visited an open day in Pounds Lane, where Cindy embarked on a meditation evening surrounded by women dressed in white, known as Sisters. Everyone was incredibly friendly and Cindy was encouraged to show one of them a postcard she carried with her that had Anne Frank's tree printed on it. Knowing she was a celebrated painter, Cindy was then introduced to Georgina Long, the Interfaith Coordinator for the organisation. They hit it off, and Cindy would join the group for meditation whenever she could. It was great to drop in as a busy mum, and leave refreshed as an artist, ready once again to start painting.

That summer, Roger and Cindy were in Paris celebrating Cindy's birthday on June 14th, when Georgina Long reached out with an invitation for them both to join her in India later that year, visiting the spiritual home of Brahma Kumaris in the national park near Mount Kumaris. The pair were over the moon to be invited and have found Georgina so kind, generous and patient throughout their whole experience. She is very special to both of them.

It took a long flight to Delhi, followed by another domestic flight and a four-hour car journey over a rocky and precarious road, Cindy had to hope that with two young sons at home, she would be safely delivered back to them – and of course, she was.

Despite being a well-travelled couple, this was a trip like no other. On arrival they were greeted with such beautiful scenery, luscious green mountains surrounded them and they were keen to get started with meditation – even though it did start incredibly early in the morning. The pair settled into a dormitory room which would be home for the next few days, although it felt to Cindy like being in a horse's stable with everyone coming and going. Roger would get up for meditation at 4am, others at 6am. There was no privacy but Cindy loved it, all the better to feel connected.

Before breakfast, everyone was encouraged to do a group meditation in the auditorium, where people from 160 different countries gathered. It was a time when anyone could grab the microphone and speak what they felt. The aim was to speak about love and happiness, to spread positivity. But one guest was so sad and when he spoke Cindy could tell he was hurting. After many years of marriage, Roger could now read Cindy so easily and held her back from wanting to run up to the stage. As soon as he let go Cindy was off, right to the front of the stage where she grabbed the microphone and said out to the two-hundred strong crowd but directed at the man,

"Why are you so angry and sad? Everyone is here today through love, and we need to appreciate the gift that we have been given. I believe that life is like a tree, and we're all the wind for each other. Ground your roots and feel safe with us, we all experience different seasons, our branches sway and our leaves fall. But overall, we need to be there for one another. Be the wind and stand tall among us."

By chance a journalist was sat next to Roger; he leaned over and asked if Cindy was a writer, after all she had such a way with words. Roger laughed warmly, always one to keep to Cindy grounded, he replied,

"Cindy? A writer? She couldn't even spell the cat sat on the mat!"

With that it was time for breakfast, a meal which was usually eaten in silence to give the participants a chance to sit and think about what they wanted to achieve from their day. Cindy always loved this experience as having a set time to be quiet helped her productivity levels and is something she still does if she gets the chance, mapping out the day ahead. Cindy explains,

"It is such a pure thing to do to eat our breakfast in silence, I'm surprised we don't have it in our schedules to sit quietly for ten minutes just to feel our heartbeat and clear our minds because we are nothing but energy. After all, you can't just keep pushing up like a car up a hill the whole time, we need rest."

After her breakfast in silence, the sound of a flautist broke Cindy's concentration and she followed everyone out of the breakfast hall and up into the rural hills. As he played, families with small children came out of their houses to look – Cindy imagined it must look like the Pied Piper leading the children over the hill, it was so quiet and serene, it was breath-taking. The flute was beautiful, and it became one of the most amazing experiences of Cindy's life. Standing on the hill, feeling the warmth of the sun and listening to the noise of the flute, Cindy almost felt as though she was back in the womb. With Cindy's talent for empathy, she has long felt that the experience of birth must be the most distressing thing that most of us ever go through. To be pushed out of our warm and cosy homes into a cold, sterile environment with bright lights – it is something that Cindy has thought about lots over the years. But this was her chance to go back there and recover from whatever trauma birth had created. For more than two hours she stood there, connected with the grid of life. It was incredible.

Most importantly, there was no pressure to be anyone but herself. No make-up required, no expensive clothes – everyone wore the same white outfits. Vegetarian food was served so that no matter our individual tastes and ideals, during that experience everyone was the same. To Cindy, it was a gift.

There was one final experience from the trip that has stuck with Cindy and resonated, her meeting with a Buddhist from Thailand. One evening he taught Cindy how to embrace transcendental meditation, the ability to move your experiences from what your body is sensing, e.g., the chair you might be sitting in or the noises you can hear around you, to somewhere else completely. To Cindy, it was like flying. It was only when she got back to England that she realised this was a rare skill, and that she was lucky to be such a natural. Cindy was in awe at the beautiful love amongst the Brahma Kumaris and how they held up each and every individual from different walks of life. She had never believed a place like this existed.

Eventually the trip came to an end, and the sheer noise and smell while in the taxi took its toll on Cindy which, after a week of peace, quiet and inner reflection, felt like an affront on her senses. But as Roger was reading in the car, he turned to Cindy, and while she was praying to God that they would get back to her children safely, he said something that Cindy has never forgotten to this day. He told her that he now knew why she had gone to acting school, and that she was fortunate that Jill had pushed her into it. Cindy was puzzled, as Roger explained that by not having to worry too much about academia, it meant that her mind remained open to new possibilities; there was nothing there to block her and so experiencing the transcendental meditation would only be an experience that someone like Cindy could take part in. It made her special.

Roger is a man of very few words, so for him to express his thoughts to Cindy in such a way was simply beautiful to her, and she knew then that she would always want to be with him.

Cindy has since worked with Brahma Kumaris to help others learn about the possibilities of meditation and spirituality, from a silenced walk to an evening of talks with other artists, Cindy enjoys being part of the sisterhood – sisterhood here is used in the loosest sense as the group is very much open to both men and women, as well as being free to the public.

In fact, Cindy was offered a larger role within the organisation, but although she was flattered, her painting and family would take precedence. However, she feels it was a great privilege to be asked.

She has since continued to paint with them whenever she has the time. In 2017 she brought her lithograph of the Anne Frank tree to share. The idea was to talk for thirty to forty-five minutes and then spend the rest of the time painting, but Cindy felt a little unusual that day. At the time she was struggling with a thyroid issue. Georgina was interviewing her, and among a packed room full of women, the pair began to talk on stage and for some reason, Cindy was unable to hold back. Out it came, the issues with the thyroid, her anger at what it was putting her through, the relationship with her mother which wasn't always perfect. Cindy didn't quite realise the impact she was having on the room until she saw one woman get up and leave. She later learned that this woman had been quite ill outside because what Cindy was saying really resonated with her.

Some of the topics Cindy touched on that day include how people perceive Cindy and how she feels judged. From suffering with dyslexia (one woman recently had the gall to say that Cindy shouldn't blame her failings on a condition that many people simply live with) to her fear of failure with not being classically trained as an artist. The occasion was one big therapy session and despite offering these women the chance to paint, they told her to carry on as they wanted to hear more about how she was feeling, as these topics were so rarely discussed despite most of the women there carrying similar emotional baggage.

When Cindy got home, she was absolutely exhausted but satisfied that many had connected with the rawness and vulnerability Cindy put out there that day. She felt so blessed and loved by the people there and to Cindy, everything happens for a reason. It was her time to receive space to deal with such long, pent up emotions and so, a great amount of healing was done. Cindy believes the universe will always give us space to heal.

CHAPTER 13

LEARNING TO TRUST HER INSTINCTS

The Golfer

Cindy has always felt that artists need some form of protection, even from themselves. Many are good and kind but have self-doubt, which means that just like Cindy did when she was starting out, they under-price and over-commit. She gives thanks that she had Roger to bounce off, someone to say "*Have you thought this through? How much will the paints cost and what about the framing?*" Without him, Cindy knows she would have made more mistakes as time is often the one thing people value least. But while Cindy has always seen the good in people, she is not naïve. Although there is only one time where she ever felt the need to take a deposit from someone. Cindy explains,

> "I had a very famous advertising agent ring me after seeing my work in The Halcyon hotel and while I have

never, ever taken a deposit from anyone, something made me ask for £1000 which afterwards, I was jolly glad I did.

"I'm always upfront with people and warn them that my paintings can take three to six months to be delivered; I paint around my life after all, and I have to find time, commission or not, to find the right mood to paint. But he would ring me every week and each phone call I received was a sure-fire way to dampen down the spirit inside of me that calms me when I paint. It got to the point where it was eating me up. I became too worried to paint – had artist's block – and the only thing I could do was to storm back into his office, walk straight past his secretary and return the cheque for his deposit. Once that man was out of my life, it became easy to paint again – exactly how it should be. And since then, I've learned to trust my gut."

While Cindy thought this would be the end of the story, she still kept his details on her mailing list as she liked to personally write when she had something upcoming of interest. Out of kindness and a wish to move on, she invited him to the Square One gallery opening, where to Cindy's surprise, he showed up. She goes on,

"He said that he wanted to buy a picture of a golfer I had painted. Straight away, I got bad vibes, and as it was a busy night, I suggested that he take it up with the manager of the gallery to arrange a meeting. Rather than lunch somewhere else, we decided to have tea in the garden the next day and talk more so that the gallerist could also keep an eye out. But once again he was so pushy that I realised he had little respect for the treasures he cultivated.

"It wasn't just that he showed up in a flashy sports car or wore a designer suit – after all, Corona trained me to work with all sorts of people – it was that he hadn't seemed to have improved since the last time he hassled me. He was very controlling. And I thought if he could do that to me, who else might he be doing it to? I'm not sure what came over me, but I told him a good few home truths and said that I wouldn't be selling the painting to him. And with that I got up and left. I'm sure deep down he's a good guy but it was just too draining for me."

He is no longer on Cindy's mailing list.

Schillings and Long

Once Cindy's artwork became popular, Cindy found a need for good friends and an even better legal team. While attending a charity event with the Duchess of York and heavily pregnant with Jack, Cindy met a couple who wanted to work with her to launch a perfume. The unassuming pair were lovely and easy to get on with, but alarm bells started to ring when the pair asked Cindy to sign some paperwork. On first glance, it looked innocent, but she was astute enough to fax it over to a 'sweet older man' she met in a coffee shop off Regent's Street, who worked at Schillings Law Firm in

London – which just so happens to be one of the top privacy and reputation legal specialists in the country. He took a look over the ten-page document which at first glance, looked very unassuming, but there were no obvious world rights.

Cindy attributes her café-acquired friend as one of her 'angels' after he confirmed that if she signed the piece of paper, the (not so innocent) couple would own absolutely everything Cindy had ever produced on paper or canvas. Even if Cindy tried to sell no more than a squiggle, they would own it for the rest of her life. Recently Cindy ran into them again and they wouldn't even look her in the eye.

Instead, Cindy decided to work out how to do things herself. Tamar Murray was a great friend who helped her put together a website and she employed Shilling and Long whenever she needed legal help, unless it was overseas. From then on, Cindy became clued-up on trademarks and copyright, making sure she owned every piece of her artwork, including the names *Celebrity Pawtraits*, the work she does for Battersea Dogs and Cats home, domain names and any and all associated world rights.

Protecting Herself

Of course, there was no better person to have in her camp than her mum, Jill. Once while away on holiday with Cindy and the family, Jill had read in the *Daily Express* paper that Lord Lichfield, the famous photographer, was going to produce a Pet Pawtraits calendar on behalf of PDSA. Cindy immediately rang Shilling and Long, who sent a long letter to the pet charity who confirmed that they wouldn't use the moniker, *Celebrity Pawtraits*. Another letter had to be sent when Cindy realised Rod Stewart's wife, Penny Lancaster, was also trying to use the name for a TV programme. While Cindy loves to support charities, she also feels it is important to keep her work under one brand, otherwise the message would become diluted, and all of her work and effort would lose its value. When Cindy does something for charity, it's her time that she gives most freely, and that is something she wants to keep sacred.

CHAPTER 14

CELEB STORIES

Unfazed by Celebrities

Cindy has had an incredible life, full of quirky experiences. Whilst some of these encounters may seem a little random, she has always been true to her heart instead of her ego and, as such, is open to all possibility. It is Cindy's belief that what we give out to the universe, we get back in spades. If, as human beings, we are positive, caring, empathetic and give to others, we will receive these qualities back in various guises. Her strength has been the ability to listen to her inner self, letting her heart and intuition guide her rather than the desire for money or self-promotion. But another one of Cindy's redeeming qualities is that she will happily talk to anyone. Celebrity or not.

Cindy's mum – who started her daughter's journey in art, after asking her to paint a picture for her new house – always advised her not to see what she does as a business, but to let go of ego and just enjoy the paths and journeys it takes her on. Whilst sometimes this can mean Cindy will turn seemingly amazing (and career-progressing) opportunities down if it doesn't feel right, doors never appear to fully close on her, and as one door starts to close, another is already opening, providing new prospects and possibilities.

Kenneth Williams

Cindy used to find herself regularly in Regent's Park when Jill lived in Bryanston Court and together they used to take out Cookie, Cindy's little Yorkshire terrier. It was here that they would bump into actor Kenneth Williams, best known for his "*Ooh matron*" catchphrase from the *Carry On* films, who lived nearby. For some reason, he didn't seem to like a lot of people, but he just loved Jill.

Once Cindy saw him while having a coffee in the café at Selfridges by herself. The way she was sitting gave her the perfect viewing position without being seen herself, and Cindy soon saw how awful it was the way people were staring at him. It gave her an early taste that fame isn't everything and that anyone could be unhappy, even celebrities. She quickly went over and spoke to him and he told her that he felt so alone. But it was only when she was able to view everyone from his point, tucked out of the way that she could see the downside to being a celebrity. Yes, we should all be flattered if we reach that station, but sometimes the experience isn't all you think it might be. This was something she never forgot throughout all the years she dealt with stars and household names. They were just people after all.

Prince Edward

Cindy was lucky enough to meet the Queen's third son, Prince Edward, a number of times in recent years. Initially at the Films Without Borders charity event to support the documentary by Jill Samuels at The Lanesborough hotel, London in 2009. It was a wonderful charity that gave children the chance to work in film. Of course, Cindy abandoned all protocol and waved at the Prince while he was on his tour around, and said "*Hi Ed, how are you?*" Once the person in charge got a whiff of it, they told Cindy that hailing the prince so informally was not allowed, but it didn't stop her.

When she saw him again for another charity event at the National Youth Theatre, she did exactly the same thing. Catherine, the Duchess of Cambridge had just had her second child, Princess Charlotte, and so Cindy chatted away about Edward becoming a great uncle again. Cindy remembers,

> "I had got it all wrong again in terms of protocol when it comes to speaking to the Royals, but after years of being on stage and working with celebrities, I don't really pay much attention to rules like that. I think it's partly to do with my dyslexia."

Nicholas Lyndhurst

One of Cindy's favourite recollections was being in a show with *Only Fools and Horses* star Nicholas Lyndhurst before he was famous. Back then he was only five years older than Cindy and was at the start of his career, working as a stagehand. Cindy remembers that she would pass him to go on stage each day, where he was dealing with the props and lights. Somehow, he had a talent to make everyone laugh as they passed him. She remembers him as a really naughty but funny guy.

Todd Carty

Another sweetheart Cindy often thinks of is Todd Carty, who had played Tucker Jenkins, the main lead in *Grange Hill*. The pair had gone on to do a film together and Cindy simply loved working with him. Once he even came back to Cindy's apartment in Bryanston Court and met her mum, Jill. She took a lovely photo together with Cindy, Todd and Cindy's dog, Cookie. Cindy says,

> "I loved acting with Todd. He was a complete natural, but around that time I realised that a career in film or on stage probably wasn't for me. But I loved the teamwork and being around the crew and everything else."

Norman Rosenthal

In 1997, there was a huge furore in the art world when the Royal Academy in London prepared to open their *Sensations* exhibition. The aim was to highlight emerging British artists from advertising mogul Charles Saatchi's personal collection.

The event was engulfed in controversy before it had even opened, due to the subject matter of many of the 110 works from forty-four young artists. They included Damien Hurst's shark suspended in formaldehyde, Tracey Emin's tent entitled *Everyone I Have Ever Slept With*, Marc Quinn's self-portrait – a frozen head made from pints of his own blood – and Jake & Dinos Chapman's porno-genetic mannequins, amongst many others. The fury the show created was unprecedented. In the UK, one of the most provocative installations was Marcus Harvey's *Myra*, an image depicting the infamous moors murderer created using children's handprints, which triggered protests, uproar and vandalism from the general public as well as upset within the art world, leading three academics to resign in disgust.

When the exhibition moved to New York, it was Christ Ofili's *The Holy Virgin Mary* from 1996 at the centre of controversy, which showed a Madonna decorated with resin-covered elephant dung and surrounded by small, collaged images of female genitalia from pornographic magazines. In a press conference at the time, Mayor Rudolph Giuliani stated the work offended him, adding that '*the city shouldn't have to pay for sick stuff.*'

There were multiple debates ongoing at the time, some believing the art world needed to move with the times and what better way than with this 'shock and awe' style tactic. Others were appalled by the themes depicted in such graphic ways within one of Britain's most iconic and beloved art institutions, and then there were the cynics who sat back to watch the spectacle unfold, secretly congratulating the academy for creating such incredible PR for the industry. The person responsible for all of this was Norman Rosenthal.

Sir Norman Rosenthal was custodian of the Royal Academy for more than thirty years. With no formal qualifications in art or art history, during his time at the Academy he helped transform it into one of the world's greatest exhibition spaces with blockbuster exhibitions, including the first show to introduce Brit art to a wider audience, the Monet exhibition in 1999 and the exhibition of 19th and 20th century masterpieces from Russian collections. Flamboyant, controversial and sometimes abrasive in nature, he was greatly admired as a cutting-edge curator. And in the late 1990s, Sir Norman just happened to be a neighbour of Cindy's.

One Sunday, whilst her children were at Hebrew School, a mutual friend suggested that Norman should visit Cindy for a tomato juice and to see her work. After admiring Cindy's *Blue and White Vase* painting, which he simply loved, they sat in her garden chatting. Norman asked if she had been to the *Sensations* show and was surprised to hear her reply in the negative. Under further questioning on the reasons why – truthfully Cindy wasn't a fan of the Chapman brother's installation and as a busy mum, she wasn't always aware of what was relevant in the art world – and so she described how she had fallen into painting, had no formal artistic background and didn't feel that comfortable with the art establishment. She explained that the principle of creating art to shock and the contrived attention the show was receiving didn't sit comfortably with her.

As always, Cindy was open and honest in her reasoning, revealing to Norman that she paints from the heart rather than for financial gain, and in admiration of both her work and refreshing way of thinking, Norman asked if she would like to be a part of the next Royal Academy Summer Show. Perhaps a little too hurriedly, Cindy politely declined as it didn't sit right with her to exhibit at the RA, although, with hindsight it would have been nice to take the children from University College Hospital to have a lovely day out at the opening of the show. Cindy relates more easily to artists like Grayson Perry, who is highly regarded within the industry but slightly unorthodox, preferring, like herself, to paint without constraint or pressure to conform to certain criteria or ideals.

Stephen Webster

In the early 1990s, one expert in fine jewellery was rising to fame – Stephen Webster – and Cindy would stare longingly through his West End shop window every time she passed. Despite her pleas and the promise of 'one day', Roger was yet to buy her his signature knuckle duster rings which would span four fingers made of 14 carat gold and dotted with Swarovski gemstones. Each ring retailed for thousands of pounds even back then.

With two amazing celebrity shows under her belt, Cindy was receiving attention from PR companies, one of which was M+M Management, a boutique agency that specialised in something called the 'bounty effect', where they would introduce one client to another in order to facilitate new business and media opportunities. Co-founder Martine Montgomery became very friendly with Cindy and was happy to invite her to an event where she would meet clients such as Tara Palmer-Tomkinson and the jeweller she had admired for so long, Stephen Webster, who was absolutely charming.

Feeling lucky and wanting to donate to a good cause, Cindy bought five lottery tickets at £50 each on the night for the strip 32-36, and to her amazement she won her very own Stephen Webster ring, donated in aid of his charity. While it wasn't a knuckle duster, Cindy was overjoyed to receive it and tracked Stephen down to say thank you. She mentioned how she was invited to an upcoming wedding that would be quite influential to his client base and so, he kindly offered to loan her a brand-new ring, necklace and earrings set.

This was a huge event of around 600 people, taking place at one of London's finest hotels, The Savoy. Perhaps the best thing about Cindy is that she rarely asks for details, and so, delighted to be wearing this new Stephen Webster jewellery set, embellished with diamonds and pearls, Cindy spent the evening enjoying herself. One spirited dancing session later however, she realised that her diamond and pearl necklace, worth around £30,000, was missing. Distraught, Cindy enlisted the help of the bridal party – much to their dismay – and a waiter eventually helped her retrieve the precious item. Still, despite the heart-stopping moment, Cindy hadn't quite learned her lesson. Roger went on to helpfully suggest that she might stay seated for the rest of the night or at the very least take off the expensive jewellery set. Not heeding his advice, it didn't take Cindy long to re-join the dancefloor for a bit of rock and roll, where she promptly lost her earrings. Once more, the guests and bridal party got down on hands and knees to find the lost items.

While most people would feel terribly embarrassed, Cindy had a good chat with the bride and smoothed over her interruption of the festivities with an invite to dinner.

Despite her adventure, she was able to return all the jewellery to Stephen and remembers the night as outrageously funny, but very bizarre.

Jimmy Choo

The same night that Cindy went to the *OK! Magazine* party with Patricia Quinn, Cindy also found herself bumping into both Stephen Webster and his wife and famous shoe designer, Jimmy Choo, who owned his own private shop designing shoes in Conduit Street. Cindy had bought numerous pairs of his shoes over the years, but was delighted to meet him in person at the event, despite originally not feeling up for going. The two spent a lot of time together and Cindy even did some matchmaking of her own, introducing both. A few weeks later, Cindy and Jimmy met for breakfast at Home House where he gave her some great advice. She remembers,

> "I had arrived in a bit of a bad mood that I couldn't shake. I was feeling hurt and revengeful of my mother-in-law, who is a very tough lady, but he gave me some wise words that I've never forgotten. He said, *"Be careful where you throw a stone in the house. Your mother-in-law might be in the bedroom, but the stone can land in the living room and hit a child."*

That resonated with Cindy, who would see the impact her parents arguing had on their children first-hand. While it's good to get things clear and out in the open, sometimes the risk of inadvertently hurting innocents is too great.

Cindy remembers Jimmy as being a very charming man who was proud of his legacy; she had a lot of time for him as he was very sweet. He even promised to make Cindy a special pair of shoes that she could take with her to go to *Celebrity Pawtraits* in New York. When Cindy heard that he had sold the name of his shoe brand in 2017, she thought it was incredible, although she knew it was his baby. Cindy believes that our names have power, a belief in numerology, and there are certain names that can add up to a Master Number. In other words, an incredibly powerful name. Jimmy Choo was one, and Cindy Lass is another.

John Stoddart

Another big event coming up in Cindy's life was her upcoming birthday. She would be turning forty and with two young children and a serious business, she often felt as though she was missing a little of herself. This came up in a conversation she had with celebrity photographer John Stoddart, who Cindy would often see at the Chelsea Arts Club. She would spend five minutes chatting with him at the bar and he would always ask what she was up to and tell her about his latest adventures. He was very keen on women wearing seamed stockings and would ask Cindy to model for him. Jokingly Cindy would turn him down but as the big birthday approached, she thought "Why not?" (Why not in italics). It would be a present to herself.

At this point in his career John had a reputation as photographer to the stars, and while none were top shelf, he was well known for his intimate portraits. Welsh actress

Catherine Zeta Jones featured in some of his sultry black and white snaps in just a bra and skirt, while fellow actress Liz Hurley posed topless. While this photoshoot would not be half as raunchy, Cindy asked a friend who owned the Soho Hotel to lend them a room for the shoot and began to look forward to it. Feeling sexy was not something that came easily to her, yet although her main feeling was of nervousness, she saw it as a challenge – something to remember. She had had to visit some rather unusual shops in Soho to find seamless stockings and a corset and so when it came to checking into the hotel it felt exciting, illicit even. Ever human, she had a slight wobble before John arrived. Wrapped only in a dressing gown, Cindy realised that actually, she didn't feel like she knew her body or what it could look like. She had been so busy with life that she lacked the time to focus on herself, something that on her own in a hotel room suddenly seemed like a huge obstacle to a sexy photoshoot. And so she rang the one person who could offer her words of comfort – Jill. A pep talk later and she strolled out to meet John, the perfect gentleman who immediately put her at ease. He showed her how to feel comfortable and pose in a more natural manner which reassured Cindy. With John in his zone behind the camera, professional and charming – he was very debonair – it made Cindy relax in front of the camera and left with incredible pictures that she is still proud of and has even showed to her sons. In fact, if presented with the opportunity again, Cindy thinks the confidence she has accumulated with age would lead to a slightly more raunchier set of snaps. She said,

"I often think that if John was able to get the best out of me that morning, then now I know and understand myself a bit better, I'd feel confident to go a little further. But it was a truly great experience, to feel so vulnerable but come out with such a good result. What a gentleman."

Barbra Streisand

When Cindy was in L.A. to unveil Anne Frank's portrait to the Museum of Tolerance, she was invited to a charity fundraising event for people in showbiz at Sunset Boulevard. Although she can't reveal too many details, it was held in the house of a famous Hollywood actress. It was here that she bumped into a good friend of Barbra Streisand's and a mutual acquaintance declared that Cindy must paint Barbra's new dog. But this wasn't just an ordinary dog; this was Samantha. A Coton de Tulear Barbra had loved so much, she had had cells taken from the mouth and stomach of the dog before she died in 2017. Streisand then went on to create two new puppies from these cells – making them clones of her original dog Samantha.

At the party, word had reached Cindy that not only had Barbra heard of her, but she loved her work and wanted to give her the commission after seeing what she had done while working on the Queen's corgis. And so, Cindy got to work on two new paintings, one of Samantha and the other of the new puppies. This time, she had only six weeks and was once again working from photos.

Having learned from her artist's block while painting Anne Frank's tree, Cindy instead embraced this deadline. There was no need to think or feel for this commission; it was simply painting – something Cindy loves the most. This time, Cindy realised that being under pressure could really bring out the best in her artwork, and although there was a lot going on at the time, the painting was one which she enjoyed.

Cindy then flew back to Santa Monica to present it to another friend of Barbra's. She was supposed to meet the renowned singer and actress in person, but unfortunately, it didn't go to plan.

Nevertheless, Cindy's care and attention was clear to see. She had the painting so well packaged that a porter had to bring his drill across to unscrew it. While Cindy did get a message from her PA that Barbra Streisand was a fan of the painting, it wasn't until she read an interview with her later on that she realised just how much. A journalist from London had gone over to interview her, and she said that she loved the painting as it really picked up the essence of Samantha.

Richard Caring

Through her charity work, Cindy has been privileged to have met a number of high-profile people in the worlds of business and celebrity. It has allowed her inside some incredible homes, like the Queen's private apartments at Buckingham Palace. At one cancer charity event, Richard Caring – a self-made multimillionaire who owns the exclusive Wentworth Golf Club and heads up Caprice Holdings (who own The Ivy chain of restaurants and private members club, Annabel's) – placed the winning bid for a pawtrait commission of his German Shepherd, Roxy.

As Cindy arrived at Richard's imposing and impressive home in Hampstead to take photographs of the dog, she was ushered into the television room where she was met by three enormous Alsatians. Trying to take photographs of the dog in question as all three milled inquisitively around her, she remembers thinking, *I am not OK.*

After 30-minutes of lying frozen on the ground she was finally rescued and had to leave with only substandard images to work from, but was struck by the palatial property with its two sweeping staircases leading to the ground floor. Cindy smiles, recounting that as the housekeeper showed her out, she commented on Cindy's unusual dog training method, not having realised Cindy was the artist not the trainer! A while after finishing the pawtrait commission, Cindy bumped into Richard Caring in her hairdresser's whilst bringing son Jack for a trim. Richard was having his highlights done. She asked him where he had put the painting and was delighted to hear it had been hung, pride of place, behind the desk in his office.

Michelle Collins

Cindy always links her career as an artist with losing out on the role of Cindy Beale in the BBC soap *EastEnders*. While it went instead to Michelle Collins, this small hiccup didn't stop them from becoming friends. In fact, Michelle was happy for Cindy to paint her Yorkshire Terrier puppy, Jemima, for Battersea *Celebrity Pawtraits*. She was delighted with the painting and came along on the opening day to make a speech and say how much she was pleased with it.

Years later, Michelle came round to Cindy's house for a family dinner just after starting her new role as Stella Price in *Coronation Street*. It was there that Jill – a massive Corrie fan yet unaware of who Michelle actually played – began to send up the programme asking if anyone had watched the new actress and wasn't she terrible, not knowing or not caring that she was actually at the table. A typical dinner with the whole family, it wasn't an easy job for an embarrassed Cindy to give Jill a little kick under the table – they were both sat someway apart from each other.

When Cindy did eventually lose her temper and blurt out that Michelle was indeed the actress in question, this faux pas didn't stop Jill in the least, who could be quite feisty; instead, she even called Michelle's accent into question. *"You must get a lot of money, can't you get some classes and do a better accent? Call yourself an actress – let's hope you get better soon!"* This horrified Cindy as Michelle was originally from Manchester, the irony of her own mother – a Coronation Street fan – threatening to boycott the show despite listening to a woman with a genuine Mancunian accent.

Cindy quickly got up and cleared the plates, mortified, but Michelle came to find her and to her credit she wasn't offended at all. *"It's OK – I love your Mum!,"* she laughed. *"Come back to the table."* Luckily by that time, the conversation had moved on and the pair have stayed friends ever since. The pair even dressed up for Halloween one year, with Michelle taking the part of the Zombie nurse. Cindy still has the picture – it was a great night.

Kevin Spacey

Cindy met actor Kevin Spacey at her son Ollie's birthday party when he turned twenty-two in 2019. An intimate gathering with family and friends, the small group were having drinks in a private room at the Chelsea Arts Club when they were told that the film star had been turned away from the private members club. Despite being in the middle of her meal, Cindy immediately sprinted after him. She remembers,

> "Without thinking I instantly legged it up the road. When I got to him I said, '*Oh I love you Kevin, don't worry about it, whatever's happened I love you. Come back and have a birthday drink.*'"

As it was the bank holiday weekend, both Kevin and his friend came back to sit with Cindy and her family; they continued to chat and drink together in the garden for hours. Kevin loved the place so much that Cindy was happy to propose him for membership there. When asked what advice he would give to Ollie and his friends in their early twenties, Kevin told them to '*Follow your heart and your passion*'. To Cindy he was quite exceptional and was part of a very magical evening that proves how life really is full of surprises.

Jenny and Tim

At other times, things just seem to happen to Cindy. Like bumping into someone and finding herself rubbing shoulders with celebs – something that happened when she met Tim Etchel.

Jenny and Tim were a cool couple, Cindy thought. Tim worked in publishing and had seen some of Cindy's work at The Halcyon hotel. So enamoured by the paintings, they made contact with Cindy for an exciting round of commissions now that their home, based in the country, was in need of some colourful artwork. On completion of these huge canvases, Cindy engineered the help of Roger's plumber Paul – who, it turned out, was extremely friendly and had previously helped her move kit back and forth to The Halycon hotel. They sat together on the long drive in his large van to deliver the paintings to the couple's countryside home.

Eventually, after several belly laughs on the journey, they arrived. Delighted with the artwork, Jenny announced they were going away for the summer, giving Cindy a set of keys so she could come and 'hang out' at their incredible property as much as she wanted. Bowled over by such a generous offer, Cindy realised this must be normal behaviour for such media folk and was hugely appreciative of the gesture, allowing herself a peek into the luxury that others often took for granted – although she never did take them up on their offer.

At the end of the summer, the exuberant couple were back in the UK and invited Cindy and Roger to a barbecue at their home in the beautiful countryside. Assuming a small, casual burgers-on-the-barbie type affair, Cindy informed her husband the dress code was 'jeans' when he asked, and she – being eight months pregnant – went as a vision of informal pink, wearing bright pink pumps and baby pink dungarees.

On arrival, they were quick to realise it was far more formal than they had anticipated, with over a hundred tables set out in an impressive marquee and catering provided by top celebrity chef of the time, Brian Turner.

What's more, the couple found themselves mingling amongst a host of A-list celebrity guests – all clad beautifully in cocktail attire; it wasn't quite the laid-back garden BBQ they were envisaging. Poor Roger was highly embarrassed, being so comparatively underdressed, but they both had a fantastic evening and Cindy loved being in her favourite maternity pink dungarees, which turned out to be a great conversation starter.

CHAPTER 15

CINDY'S CHARITY EXPERIENCES

Cindy has always confronted the good and the bad in people and while she would be the first to admit that Jill was impatient and sometimes selfish, this upbringing allowed Cindy to find her own charitable spirit. She grew up watching her mum frequenting charity benefits and other glamorous events yet Jill also always made sure to buy individual Christmas presents for all the people in her life – even the porter. And so, Cindy would always do her best to help when requested – whether that was donating a painting for auction, helping out behind the scenes or creating an invite or a logo. Sometimes, Cindy would head to a charity lunch or gala dinner without even knowing much about the cause she was trying to help. One such time they arrived at Somerset House in Aldwych where a presentation began on the perils pregnant young African women faced giving birth. The talk was graphic and upsetting, despite sitting at the back Cindy had to walk out.

She was grateful that her painting would raise much needed funds to tackle such awful problems in the world, but with such strong empathetic skills, she had to protect her own emotional stability or she might never get out of bed.

Chai Cancer Care

One charity that has stayed close to Cindy's heart is Chai Cancer Care, the Jewish community's national cancer support organisation. Cindy has visited their facilities numerous times, but on the first occasion back in 2014, Cindy was asked to submit a painting that could be auctioned on an upcoming spa day. She was also asked to bring with her another painting that she had begun and that the patients could finish with help. On a bright sunny day in the garden, Cindy really connected with these beautiful souls, who for a brief afternoon found as much joy in painting as she did.

A few months later, Cindy returned to another facility to paint with the patients themselves. It took some time, but once Cindy had them put their handbags down, it humbled Cindy how so many wanted to get involved. She said,

"It was hard for some of them to just get up and paint. Many turned towards me and said, '*What should I do?*' With all their troubles you could see they were uptight, so I stood behind them and got them to relax. Once they understood the task, it was hard to pull the paintbrush away for the next person to try it! It seems like suddenly they had stepped through to the unknown and that was it, I couldn't get them away."

Queen's College Visit

Another time after meeting someone from a commission, she was asked to open an art gallery of the children's work at the Queen's College in Marylebone. Cindy loves going into schools to talk to children, so she was thrilled to oblige. Before the opening she had a chance to say hello to the headmistress and "thanks for having me" – but unbeknown to Cindy, the headmistress was familiar with the lithograph of the Anne Frank tree, which was hanging in New Cavendish Street, just around the corner, and she mentioned it while introducing Cindy, saying,

> "To have a well-known living artist out there open the children's art show is very impressive for them."

Cindy was shocked and flattered, she had been running around all day and hadn't really had a chance to take it in. But when she got up on stage to talk to the audience, she soon realised that she recognised half the mums and dads there, so her poise was quick to return and the Corona confidence came back.

The National Holocaust Museum

With Cindy dedicating so much time and focus to Anne Frank, she was touched when The National Holocaust Museum reached out to see if they could collaborate. Cindy had heard the story of some remarkable brothers, Stephen and James Smith, who had gone over to Israel in their early twenties where they felt moved by the suffering of Jews at the World Holocaust Remembrance Centre. Concerned that there was no national effort in England to help or lend their attention too, the boys started to use rooms in their own house to preserve important British connections to the Holocaust. Over time, work was done on the site in Laxton, Nottinghamshire and it now employs around thirty people with a small army of volunteers, including Holocaust survivors who do daily talks to the approximately 30,000 annual visitors, many of them school children.

Cindy had been asked by the board to create a painting so that they could raise money from the sale. Cindy painted a white rose that was studded with Swarovski crystals and jumped on the train to Nottingham with her two sons to present it. Cindy remembers being incredibly moved on her journey around the museum; they listened to a Holocaust survivor and touchingly, Cindy remembers welling up at a huge pile of buttons that represented all the family members that had been lost.

Now hung in the museum, she knew that the effort of the two brothers to dedicate their life to such work was very special indeed and she was happy to support it.

Most Expensive Painting

Most adventures for Cindy seem to start on a night in the company of Patricia Quinn and this one is no exception. The pair were drinking and dancing away at the Royal Academy of Arts when Cindy felt a craving for a cigarette. She had stopped previously and so hadn't any on her.

She crossed the road to the restaurant Cecconi's and asked if it would be possible to borrow one from two Scottish women who were sat eating outside. They kindly said yes and after a quick chat, one of the women made her excuses and left.

The talk turned to jobs and Cindy explained she was an artist. The woman then turned to Cindy and told her that her boss, who had just left, had a son who was dreadfully ill with epileptic fits and they were trying to raise the money for a portable machine which was very expensive. There was already an auction planned at the Dorchester and would it be possible for Cindy to auction off a pawtrait? Cindy said of course, she left her number and they sorted it all out the next day. While Cindy couldn't go personally to the event, she received a phone call the next day that said her work had started a bidding war. The number had reached £9,000 before the person running the auction intervened and promised a painting each if they were both happy to commit the money. Of course, Cindy felt she could only agree to this, even though it was slightly unprecedented, but £18,000 would go a long way to help to raise the funds required. Plus, Cindy was flattered that as a relatively unknown artist, her work was commanding such figures.

One of the winning bidders was a lady she arranged to meet on New Kings Road after promising her she would paint her three dogs on canvas. She wasn't from London and lived on a farm just outside, and as a thank you for Cindy she turned up with boxes of various eggs, from duck eggs to chicken. That simple act of kindness was hugely appreciated by Cindy and it's moments like that when she feels blessed to be giving her time to charities.

The Red Cross

Over time Cindy has found herself on lots of committees, whether it's to create guestlists or source prizes. But on one of her first committees, she was asked to create a design for the exclusive Red Cross Ball on the 13th of June 1998. Momo would be doing the food and it was to be held at the Windsor Polo Club. While Cindy had made a start, she was a busy woman and so the painting had fallen down the to-do list when she received a phone call – was it finished yet? It was at that point Cindy realised that although the ball itself was far enough away, her painting was going out in the middle of the invite, not just an auction prize. And so, it needed to be printed immediately. With that in mind Cindy sat down and got on with it. She remembers,

> "The ball was Morocco-themed, and I thought I had plenty of time to do it, but it turned out it was only around four weeks. Originally it was supposed to be on the programme which was why I put it to the back of my mind, but they actually used it for their invitations, which with a mailing list of 20,000 was a big deal. Thank God they loved it!"

Terrence Higgins

In 2001, Cindy was approached by the Terrence Higgins Trust to paint a piece for the Ralph Lauren Lighthouse Auction at a famous auction house. Having just given birth to her second son Jack, and once again having her house overrun with builders working on the property, it was a chaotic period. Needed at home to oversee the construction, care for her new baby and older son, she longed for a day where she could sit in the garden and escape for a few hours. It was this desire for nature, distraction and wanting to be anywhere but where she was that led Cindy to paint *Summer Breeze* for the charity auction. It represented a daydream ideal of sitting in a beautiful garden on a summer's day with unbroken blue skies, blossom gently waving in the light breeze, whilst drinking a cup of tea, a sumptuous bowl of cherries on the table waiting to be tucked into. At a time when she was feeling caged in, it helped to free her mind by painting this wonderful picture, reminiscing on times she 'loved to sit and watch the world go by from a simple wooden bench in sunny Primrose Hill'. She remembers:

> "Those carefree days, spent connecting with myself, listening to the beautiful birds and feeling the summer breeze."

It's something that would resonate with any new mother remembering the days before children. Cindy loved the painting and what it symbolised for her, but was nervous about the auction; would anyone else understand what she was trying to convey? With other high-profile lots selling for the charity, Cindy felt a bit of pressure and unease in case her painting didn't sell for a cause she felt strongly about. She need not have worried; the auction was a resounding success and her painting sold for £3,200, raising more funds than an original from Prince Charles which was next on the lot, right after her painting. Waiting to see if *Summer*

Breeze would outsell the future monarch's own painting was nail-biting for Cindy, and the joy when realising that her own work had sold for more brought a quiet sense of achievement.

Watts Gallery – An Immersive Prison Experience

Relying on an intuitive feeling isn't always an easy process. Cindy recalls supporting her friend and actress Jenny Seagrove, who had helped by opening *All Our Hearts Beat As One*. Jenny had her own charity, Mane Chance, a sanctuary that would rescue neglected and abandoned horses and ponies, bringing them back to health both physically and emotionally. In turn, the horses go on to provide therapeutic benefits to visiting children with disabilities and terminal illnesses. Cindy had been asked to donate a painting in 2014 for a fundraising event which she did with pleasure.

Each year Jenny runs a hugely successful Christmas lunch and on this occasion, Cindy was able to join her at the top table. She began chatting to a very well-spoken lady at the next table. She introduced herself as Perdita Hunt, the director of Watts Gallery, which was situated very close to the Mane Chance horse sanctuary just outside Guildford in a village called Compton. Perdita explained that she was heavily involved through the art gallery with community projects and, in particular, guiding and teaching art to female offenders. This was something that really pulled at Cindy, as something she wanted to get involved in. And so, she jumped at an invite to come and see the gallery and Perdita arranged for her to give a talk at the prison.

Since 2008 the Watts Gallery Trust has been providing regular workshops for these women to create their own work in a studio facilitated by the artist in residence who supports and mentors them. Thereafter their work is submitted to competitions and exhibitions and every year their work is exhibited in *The Big Issue Exhibition* at Watts Gallery.

Cindy arrived bright and early at HM Prison Send on the morning of her talk, but it wasn't until she was going through the many security checks that it dawned on her – she was going to be locked in a room with some serious offenders. There were three prison officers and eight women prisoners, but once Cindy was introduced and had begun her presentation, she was able to relax into the situation.

It was a fascinating day – what she had thought would be a thirty-minute demonstration turned into three hours of engaged conversation, chat and painting. One of the prisoners took a particular interest and Cindy felt a genuine chill run down her spine. There was something about this female prisoner, who to protect her identity will be referred to as Jane Doe, that made her blood run cold. Cindy was never one to judge a book by its cover; she knew nothing about the women in the room – neither full names or the crimes they had committed – not one thing that could sway her subconscious view even remotely. But there was just something about Jane that felt different from the others. Shuddering at the recollection, Cindy says:

"It was the first time I had actually seen energy come from a person, and it was black energy."

Jane kept asking questions about Cindy's emotions – "*How did you feel when your paintings were sold?*" – normal questions but from her it felt strange and unsettling. Later in the discussion, Jane wanted to show her work to Cindy and so needed to return to her cell. Two guards immediately sprang up to escort her, and it was then that Cindy registered just how dangerous Jane might be.

Cindy was eventually allowed to leave her *All Our Hearts Beat As One* badges that all included a small pin – the guards were initially worried they could have been used as a sharp weapon. But Cindy did keep in touch with the scheme and was able to secure a job for one of the women once she left the facility.

Exhilarated but exhausted after the mammoth coaching session at the prison, Cindy couldn't shake off the feeling she'd experienced with Jane. It made her feel uncomfortable, unclean even, so she made herself a hot Epsom Salts bath to cleanse away the bad energy. Having now been told the prisoner's full name, she was telling her son, Jack, about this particular prisoner, unaware that he was quickly able to locate the full horrors of her crime via an online search engine.

As Jack began to read out the information he was discovering online, Cindy leapt out of the bath and immediately slammed the laptop shut. She didn't want to hear any more. Perhaps there was something sinister behind her inquisitive behaviour that day or maybe – as Cindy preferred to view it – Jane was in the process of working on herself and looking for a better version, answers to questions about who she was and why.

Unfortunately, Cindy couldn't make the opening of the Watts Gallery Show – something she was very sorry about because she wanted to show support for the women's achievements – but she did pop down to Surrey a few days later to visit the gallery and see the prisoners' handiwork. It made fascinating viewing. She couldn't help but notice that one of Jane's pieces of art was a heart created out of pipe cleaners entitled *Feelings of a Heartbeat* – in fact, everything was to do with feelings and the heart – strange when the badge she had left featured the logo for *All Our Hearts Beat As One*. She later learned that Jane's work was chosen to feature in exhibitions for other galleries, such as the Mall Galleries near Buckingham Palace. Cindy realised in amazement that actually, despite being in prison, it was still possible to be a sought after, collective artist.

Facemasks

Cindy's charitable arm has continued throughout the global pandemic. After printing the Queen's corgis on facemasks during the pandemic to sell from her online shop, Cindy made sure that the 600 went to a charity called Chickenshed, which supports disabled children by teaching them to dance and act.

Cindy also donated more corgi facemasks to Battersea Dogs and Cats Home. Cindy says,

> "When I sent that box of facemasks to Battersea it felt like I was going full circle as that was where I started with *Celebrity Pawtraits*. But honestly, it's great to see that they're doing really well with a big celebrity base raising funds for them. I'm so proud of what they have achieved."

Portraits

Cindy has never looked to do portraiture, although she admires many artists who do. Eventually Cindy was worn down by a friend's husband who asked her to paint his family of four. But as families tend to do, a year later it had grown and so Cindy was asked to add a third child. Cindy explains,

> "Try as I might when I went to add the third child I couldn't get the co-ordination of the paint colour right on his face. It certainly wasn't my finest work and I have never done a portrait since – only a pawtrait! Luckily, they all laugh about it now but it was an interesting journey – such is life!"

Lockdown cooking

During the pandemic Cindy found that cooking was the only thing that helped her continue her meditative state. Based in London where there were lots of good causes and charities to work with, it would not only give Cindy joy to cook for others, but she found it easy to share with neighbours who didn't have as much. Like most of her outings, Cindy would bump into someone in street one day and form a tight bond very quickly. The next day, they would have one of Cindy's specials on the table. Cindy says:

> "My speciality is known as the Cindy escalope; I make my own bread crumbs and it gives me such

a joy to share my food. Kindness and cooking have been a great leveller for me in this covid situation alongside my dog, family and friends."

While the global pandemic has given Cindy time to sit and think about the mark she has made on the art world, it certainly doesn't feel like a place to end her work. For Cindy, this is more like the beginning. Only this time, without the stress of motherhood and a much-revived purpose, Cindy gets to decide exactly what the future holds.

EPILOGUE

FROM CINDY TO YOU

And just like that, my book is over.

While there have been plenty of opportunities to tell my story over the years, I wanted to make sure that the timing was right. Meeting Gina Clarke and having her hold my hand, allow me to dip in and out while understanding me and letting me leave voice messages where I can. I'm so grateful to her that she wanted to share my story and that we have forged a great connection. I know this is not the end of what we will do together. For a long time, I used to look at my paintings and think, *me? An artist?* But I've started to realise I only admit to being an artist through my temperament. I really dislike labels however, this is the life we live in. My grandma used to say as you are one to seven years old in Yiddish as you are in life and she was right! That's why I try and collect a piece of my artwork from each 'stage' in my life. Whether it's exploring the texture of acrylic, the pressure of a deadline or simply painting through my grief like when my dad was in hospital. Each painting represents a different part of 'Cindy' and I'm so grateful to have them in my life.

Truly this book has been a journey for me. Not only did I go into it with a passion to tell the truth, but it has allowed me to feel much more connected to the people I have discussed. I have felt many times that my dad has visited me while writing this book and although my mother unfortunately died before it was published, her strike while the iron is hot attitude really got me over the finishing line. Not forgetting that Roger's stability and support have always been so welcome – and of course, my little dog Flash who at twelve years old unfortunately passed away on March 28th, 2022. Throughout the last 13-years and each difficult moment, there was one little four-legged friend who woke me up in the morning and gave me a new breath of fresh air to go out and greet the world with – whatever it held. There wasn't one day that I didn't walk Flash, whether in Regent's Park or Primrose Hill and feel my heart lift. It was like being hugged, a thousand billion times. He was the best companion I could have asked for and while the void in my heart is beyond breaking, at least I know he is not suffering anymore. I couldn't have done this without him. He had been my constant companion after Cookie and Ralph and I am so grateful to have his very own pawtrait on my wall. Having my boys, Ollie and Jack, watch and react to the various projects and stages I've been through has given me the hug I need to see things forward on my journey; they have been so supportive. My boys (sons) are my best creations EVER and painfully my best teachers. Explaining how I feel about something doesn't make it right, other opinions have to be listened to with an open ear and patient mind (I'm still working on this). I still find it a miracle that they came out of my stomach, they joined Roger and I together and we all have a strong bond still today. As they say we are work in progress...

I am lucky enough to be in touch with my own higher self, and when my mother completed her last moments in late 2021, I had the most amazing experience of seeing her pass and it only cemented my feelings on life, energy and how manifesting can actually help people. My mother was so stylish, she dressed well right up until the last moment. Even though she was thrown in the deep end with a strong mother of her own and a strong husband, my father, she stood by who she was and I have huge respect for that. She knew what she liked and she stuck to it. She would often say the Yiddish expression *Beshert*, which means *destiny*. She never shied away from the difficult things in life ever. There was only one Jilly Grant, her motto was Live Well, Laugh Often, Love Much. Overall, I have enjoyed being my mother's daughter, even though I found it painful at times, because she pushed me to find my power and strength, whether she understood it or not.

I have never been one for school or education, however, a disciplined mind is of course important and everyone absorbs information differently. I'm still a firm believer that we need to respect our space and who we share it with, whether it be animals or plants. And that if we put our own positivity out there, then it will be returned ten-fold. We're told that life has a start, a middle and a finish, but it's how you run the race that counts – the journey. As a cook myself, I see it as baking a cake; it isn't always about the ingredients you put in, but the love and care you show it. You can just tell when something has been made with love, and that makes all the difference.

Sometimes I think that painting was the only option for me, something I found at a time when I felt lost and lonely. Other members of my family who have gone through a similar situation have turned to other, more unhealthy outlets, such as gambling. And that could have easily been me. Which is why I want to spread the word that art is a healer, or just living with positive thoughts. How you talk to yourself is very important. And just like what I did with *All Our Hearts Beat As One*, we need to come together through art to spread that positivity. Now, I finally feel at a stage in my life where I want to physically help people. Not just through charity and auctioning off my paintings or volunteering my time, but actively getting involved. To that, all I would say is watch this space and give give me a like or a follow on social media to see what comes next. I have big plans and certainly feel that, right now, the world needs a sprinkle of creativity.

My work is to be enjoyed. And going back to my love of colour, it doesn't matter how people react to my paintings because I've done my job, which is to be honest with my feelings. That has then been translated onto the page and painted by my hand. I still can't get over the fact that people really like my paintings. But there is so much negativity in this life and we are taught to critique from such a young age. For me, there is no better simple pleasure than walking hand in hand with my husband; it's one of the most sweet and intimate things we can do. But I do fear that we are losing the meaning of intimacy, and with my boys now all grown up, sometimes I am worried for this next generation where nothing is private.

Throughout all the awful things that have happened to me, my miscarriage, my darling mummy's death and my dear daddy passing a while ago, I believe these have tested my sanity and judgement of myself and are making me a better and stronger woman. But I got through it by believing that tomorrow would be a better day and kept on being kind to people even though at times I wanted to scream. Mum always said reach for the moon and you'll touch the stars. We're all in this together, and it helps to know that everything is changing, always.

Take away from this book that your time is your own. Use it wisely to bring joy to yourself. Don't feel forced or pressured to make art for art's sake. Enjoy it, however you get there. Right now, we've been given a pause button, and for me, I've taken this time to understand where I'm going. Because there's no turning back, just like when I committed to paint that first ever painting for Barbara Grundy at Ebury Street. I had no idea where life would take me. And it's scary that I'm sharing my feelings with everyone through canvas, but as I've done gallery show after gallery show over the years, the biggest thing I enjoy is watching someone smile when they see my art. That it reminds them of a carefree, childlike time.

We all need that breathing space to enjoy life. So, I hope that this book inspires you to pick up a pen, pencil, brush, needle or whatever you need to create. Go. Be free. Be positive. And most of all, be colourful. Be the best person – who you really are – from the inside out. XXX

SOCIAL MEDIA LINKS

If you'd like to find out more about what Cindy Lass does next, you can find her at:

Online: www.cindylass.com
Facebook: www.facebook.com/cindy.lass.35
Instagram: www.instagram.com/cindy_lass_
TikTok: www.TikTok.com/cindy888artfromtheheart
Twitter: www.twitter.com/cindylass1

TRIBUTES

Andrew Coningsby – Founder and MD – Début Art
& The Coningsby Gallery, London W1.

I met Cindy in the 1990s and was excited to help her with her first solo exhibition in my gallery. The work was bold, colourful and beautiful and the exhibition launched a thousand ships for her!

Cindy is a high energy individual with a warm and caring heart who has gone on to initiate many great and diverse ventures for the betterment of others. I'm looking forward to catching up with her in London soon.

Jenny Seagrove

Cindy's art is life-affirming! It is both naïve in the art sense and joyous and she leads by example with her concept of *All Our Hearts Beat as One.*

Tamar Murray

I have been around the world several times and visited many museums and art galleries but Cindy Lass never ceases to amaze me.

I have to say I am proud to have her paintings hanging on my walls and have great admiration for this self-taught artist and her causes, which are many.

She captures the essence of the subject she is painting every time and does so with love and exuberance.

Meg Matthews

I love Cindy's work it makes me smile and be happy, how she captures trees, flowers, and dogs in her own personal way which is unique and different. And she does what she loves with no conforming just what she feels, when she is painting this shines through. Art From The Heart sums it up in one line, go check her out today.

Jackie St Clair

I love the tulips I bought in 1995, Cindy's unique naive style brings a smile to my face.

I've had lots of lovely comments since I bought the painting.

Nick Waters

Cindy and her art are unique. With bold brush strokes and a riot of colours she captures the spirit of her subjects. Her pawtrait of my Irish Water Spaniel 'Star' makes me smile every time I look at it.

Christopher George of Frame Designs

While researching this book, Cindy discovered the sad news that Barbara Grundy had died several years ago. However, she was able to get in touch with Christopher George of Frame Designs, which, when opened in 1985, used to be Living Interiors at 57 Ebury Street and was Barbara's neighbour for over two decades. He recalls:

> "When I arrived, Barbara Grundy was next door at 59 Ebury Street. She put on exhibitions, featuring artists that she came across several times a year, and the framing side ran throughout each year. She also rented a basement across the road in Ebury Street where a lot of the framing was carried out.
>
> "Barbara was a very vivacious lady with red hair. I do recall her telling me that she had come across a would-be artist by the name of Cindy Lass, who painted colourful pictures, and I think Barbara put on an exhibition featuring several artists.
>
> "All I can tell you about Barbara is that she was always very interested in art and was married to Lionel Grundy, who was Senior Police Advisor,

Inspector of General Police, Dependent Territories. They had two daughters, Claire and Katherine and lived down in Wiltshire.

She eventually had to give up the business and I bought it off her and have run the picture-framing business (as Frame Designs) ever since from No. 57 Ebury Street."

Empty or not, Cindy will always find herself drawn to 59 Ebury Street where her career began, all thanks to Barbara Grundy, a guardian angel for artists who lacked confidence.

CINDY'S THANKS

I would like to end this book with my own thank-you's to the people who have helped me along the way – to choose my path, plot a new course when needed and sometimes, even right the ship.

Of course, top of the list is a big thank you to the people that helped start this book. Nicole Lampert Brockman, thank you for being so wonderful and inviting me to drinks to launch your new Facebook group. If I hadn't have gone I would never have met Gina.

Gina – wow, what a journey! A busy mum with two young children, thank you for your patience and wanting to share my story and encourage people of all ages to believe in themselves. Whether to paint, cook or just to love. Thank you for writing my story.

My life wouldn't have been the same without my parents. I've spoken a lot about my mummy but my dad Jack was also one of my favourite people. My memories are of going ice skating on a Sunday morning with him, burning the leaves in the garden or collecting conkers with my brother and sister on The Bishop's Avenue.

Dad had tremendous patience and was generous beyond his lifetime. He always used to pick me up from school and then when he was semi-retired he used to pick me up from parties. And my Mum and Dad bought me a beautiful pink bike and he taught me how to ride it. I'll never forget him.

I vividly remember happy times in White Lodge Close and they were made all the sweeter by a beautiful family who lived opposite us, the Simpson's. Jane who was like a second Mum to me, and even now I can't eat roast chicken without her delicious homemade bread sauce to go with it. There was always an invite to Sunday lunch if I was around! Jane was a great friend to my mother and all my family. Her kindness still runs through my veins, she's a beautiful soul and I'm still friendly with her daughter Emily. I feel very blessed to know her.

My whole life I've been surrounded with strong, female characters to look up to and my grandma Sarah Simpkin was a great example. She lived to 102 and worked for the Russian government. She decided that she didn't want to get engaged, and instead made my grandpa wait until she was thirty. She said sometimes the wheels of life turn slowly and you've just got to hang in there – I love that expression. Aged ninety she told me that if you can't be a best friend to yourself then you're no good for anyone and five years ago I really felt that. Both sets of grandparents came from Poland and Russia, and certainly I've often felt vulnerable due to my roots, a sympathy I share with countless others.

On to my path to become an artist and I would like to thank my angels, each one has been a stitch to the big, big picture. Obviously, Barbara Grundy and Andrew Coningsby who started out my career, Professor Stan Smith and all the other people I've mentioned in the book. But a huge, huge hug goes to my mummy in heaven for being a brilliant critic and support through dark and difficult times.

After Coningsby, everything got really busy. But my mum told me to not get stressed about commissions, she said *"It's very rare you enjoy something – please don't make it a business"*. I've followed that path ever since.

My dear friends for helping me to live this crazy life.

Larraine Krantz for being a true friend, grounding me emotionally. Her saying is sit through the eye of the storm and it's done me well.

Adam Wilkie for always believing in me and listening and also my friend Ruti Verity.

Karina and Becky for not only giving me your gallery space for All Our Hearts Beat As One in 2012 and 2016 but doing absolutely everything to put it on. From invitations to brochures to artists etc. I truly appreciate it.

My thanks also go to Talia Santino for the crystal grid and Darren James for the Cacao medication experience during the 2016 event. It was amazing. My new friends and healers Michala Wellington and Alessandro Laganá who have been wonderful to heal me throughout my recent illnesses.

Annabelle Schild for supporting and sponsoring All Our Hearts Beat As One (I know you wanted to be kept unmentioned in the background but I had to mention you for all your kindness and generosity and how you want the world to be a more happy and peaceful place for the next generation).

Carolyn Rodney, the amazing lady who introduced me to Roger and her now husband Steve Bernstein – she was a big momentum in my life.

Heather Nova who in 2005 met me for an E and O dinner and realised I channelled and held me through a dramatic conversation with our waiter. She started me on my spiritual journey.

My mother-in-law for never believing in me and for my husband, her son, and my sons who always have.

There is one woman who has definitely stood out and taught me so much about myself and fear. That is Nikki Boughton, now Nikki Newman. I knew her from Corona. Wow, even my Mum loved her too! A lady with love, integrity and who never moves the goalposts. She co-ordinated my 2016 show with 55 celebrities and 60 artists and without her, trust me, I couldn't have done it. She tells me the truth on any situation, and has inspired me to becoming the big, strong woman that I am today.

And Tamar Murray who from day one of meeting me just understood my character and when I casually said to her as we were going in to play tennis (which she thrashed me at), *"Oh I'm going to do a painting and have an art show"*, she said *"Brilliant! I know you're going to be great at whatever you do"*. Whenever I've seen her she's always complimented and supported me. And you will need people like that around you in life. So, thank you Tamar Murray for bringing sunshine, and always being there for me. She taught me how to use emails and explained how important they were going to be – how right she was! More to the point she has always believed in everything I have ever done and loved me unconditionally.

To the people I have met through the opportunities and experiences I've been a part of along the way, I'm so glad to have known you.

Eva Schloss told me once how her brother and father had keeled over marching their way to freedom out of the concentration camps – almost at liberation. I asked, *"Don't you hate Hitler and the Nazi's for what they did?"* But her stepfather Otto Frank had told her not to carry on hating as it means the story continues. To get on with your life and move forward is the only way to end it – I thought that was a really mature way to look at things.

To Jenny Seagrove for introducing me to new opportunities. What I loved about Watts Gallery was the artist there in the 1800s got all the people in the village to help him. George Frederick Watt is considered to be our greatest artist from the Victorian era and his wife Mary was a pottery artist. The couple encouraged villagers to help them build and paint a nearby chapel and eventually opened their own gallery to display John's work. I found it brilliant to work with Watt's Gallery and found great comfort in the work they do to bring art into prisons.

I learned that one of the ladies from the prison that I painted with actually achieved a new start in life and now has a successful career. Now I call that a really successful day. To be locked in a room for three hours might sound scary but it really invigorated me. Not only could I talk to the women, but it gave me a great opportunity to spend time painting and see their work. Some of them were brilliant artists – much better than me!

I have to remind myself that the kindness we show ourselves is how we can show kindness to others. Learning to live with a chatterbox mind can be difficult but if we don't judge ourselves then we certainly can't judge others. We're brought out of a warm, watery womb into dryness, bright lights and noise – and from that day our journey starts. But as long as you're on the journey, you're alive.

My heartfelt message to you the reader is, if it feels right – do it. Enjoy.

To all those who I didn't mention – the list really would be too long. Thank you. You know who you are.

And finally, these last few years I have had six very special friends of mine who have passed away, the void is huge. Henry Cummings, Victoria Hyman, Russel Ereira, Lawrence Gilmore, Susan Vanner, Ruth Kaye – I know they are all doing wonderful things on the other side however, my heart goes out to all their family and friends who miss them beyond words. As do I.

This book is printed on paper from sustainable sources managed under the Forest Stewardship Council (FSC) scheme.

It has been printed in the UK to reduce transportation miles and their impact upon the environment.

For every new title that Matador publishes, we plant a tree to offset CO_2, partnering with the More Trees scheme.

For more about how Matador offsets its environmental impact, see www.troubador.co.uk/about/